bigCat diary Leopard

Leopard

Jonathan and Angela Scott

Collins

To Pam Savage, for her many kindnesses.

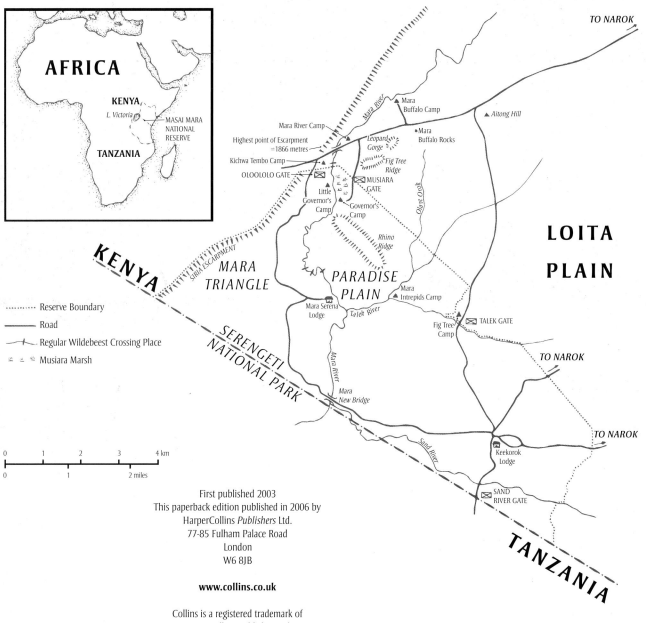

First published 2003
This paperback edition published in 2006 by
HarperCollins *Publishers* Ltd.
77-85 Fulham Palace Road
London
W6 8JB

www.collins.co.uk

Collins is a registered trademark of
HarperCollins *Publishers* Ltd.

11 06 08 09 07 10 12

10 9 8 7 6 5 4 3 2 1

© 2003 Jonathan and Angela Scott

ISBN 0 00 721181 3

Edited by Caroline Taggart
Designed by Liz Brown

Colour reproduction by Colourscan, Singapore
Printed and bound in Singapore

Contents

Introduction

> *Hawks for sunlight; owls for half-light; but for the night, cats, wild cats.*
>
> Doris Lessing: On Cats

When *Big Cat Diary* was first commissioned in 1996, we imagined it would be a one-off, stand-alone series. Surely a follow-up that again featured lions, leopards and cheetahs in the Masai Mara in Kenya would seem repetitive. 'Not another lion hunt or wildebeest river crossing,' we could hear people groaning. But we were wrong. The response to the first series was so positive that in September 1998 we returned to the Mara to film a second.

The challenge was to make it feel different. We would still concentrate most of our efforts on finding and filming the three big cats, but would also include material on some of the Mara's other resident characters, such as the spotted hyenas, jackals and elephants. We knew that people identified strongly with the

The best times to look for predators are dawn and dusk. The Mara is an ideal place to view big cats, due to the open, rolling terrain.

individual cats, so we wanted to provide as much continuity as possible. By returning to the Musiara Marsh area in the northern Mara we felt confident we could find the cats we had filmed in the previous series. As in the first series, co-presenter Simon King followed the cheetahs, I searched for leopards, and we both covered the lions.

Because Angie and I live in Kenya and spend long periods of time on safari as wildlife photographers in the area surrounding Musiara Marsh, we are in the ideal position to help keep track of our animal stars between series, relying heavily on the co-operation of our friends among the drivers and guides at the various camps

A lioness stares out across Musiara Marsh, the heart of the Marsh Pride's dry-season territory.

Half-Tail and Zawadi when she was nine months old, walking along Fig Tree Ridge early one morning, looking for a place to lie-up for the day.

and lodges. Drivers from Governor's Camp (which is situated in the Musiara area) keep a daily game record, noting which lions, leopards and cheetahs they have seen, what they killed and any other interesting details. Over the years they have named key geographical features, creating an unofficial 'map' that everyone who knows the area understands, making it relatively simple to guide vehicles to a sighting of lions or a leopard. Whenever we visit the Mara we meet the drivers and go through the game record, catching up on all the news. My association with the Mara's big cats goes back over 25 years, to the time when Brian Jackman and I wrote a book entitled *The Marsh Lions*, detailing the life of a pride whose territory centres on Musiara Marsh and about which Angie and I have kept records ever since.

When you see a pride of lions slumped in the shade of an acacia tree, an amorphous mass of tawny hides intertwined in friendly union, it seems impossible to distinguish one from another.

Over time Angie and I have learned to recognize each cat as an individual, marked out by its unique character and physical presence. But in order to be absolutely certain who is who, we rely on the lion's whisker-spot pattern, which remains constant throughout its life. Though we know each lion by name – Notch, Scar, Brown Mane, Khali – we generally avoid using these names on *Big Cat Diary*. To the audience one lion looks much the same as the next – at times they do to us, too – so naming them all would simply add to the confusion. Instead we focus on the story of the pride, and in this respect the Marsh Lions have provided a sense of continuity, playing a leading role in each of the four series filmed to date.

The spotted cats have proved somewhat easier to identify for the audience, particularly the leopards. Half-Tail, our all-time favourite, became an instant star of the first series, her short stumpy tail simply adding to her character. Leopards are normally shy and retiring, spending much

of their time hidden from view, so being able to work with Half-Tail was a joy, in marked contrast to my first years in the Mara, when it was virtually impossible to see a leopard. For as long as Half-Tail was alive we could almost guarantee finding her somewhere among the acacia country surrounding Leopard Gorge and Fig Tree Ridge, to the north-east of the Marsh. During that first series, Half-Tail was accompanied by a seven-month-old cub whom the drivers named Zawadi, meaning 'gift' in Swahili (to the television audience she is known as Shadow, though I always think of her as Zawadi). A leopard with a young cub ensured that there was plenty of activity for us to film, and as these were the only leopards we featured there was never any doubt as to who they were.

In 1996 Simon had two female cheetahs to work with, each with young cubs. He named the adults Fundi (the specialist) and Kidogo (the small one). Two years later the cheetah story became even easier to tell. For many years the drivers and safari guides had kept track of a female they had named Queen, due to her regal bearing. Queen didn't have cubs when we filmed the first series, but she must have given birth a few months later, because by the time we returned she was accompanied by three large cubs. Simon preferred the name Amber to Queen, acknowledging her beautiful amber eyes. Though each cheetah has a unique pattern of spots there was never any chance of mistaking Amber. She was so relaxed around vehicles that she often leapt up onto the bonnet. There was nothing playful or pet-like about her behaviour – she simply treated vehicles as just one more termite mound, an aerial perch from which to peruse her surroundings. Amber's cubs soon learned to be equally fearless of vehicles, though they preferred to jump up onto the spare tyres on the back of the cars and then hop up onto the roof, much to the delight of visitors, who were treated to a unique close-up view of these beautiful creatures.

As filming of the second series drew to a close we once again found ourselves wondering if there would be another. It brought back memories of the time when Brian Jackman and I were working on *The Marsh Lions*, and people kept asking us why we were producing yet another book on lions. Surely Joy Adamson's landmark tale *Born Free*, narrating the story of Elsa the lioness in the wilds of Kenya, had said all there was to say. And if it hadn't, then what about George Schaller's treatise *The Serengeti Lion*, for anyone looking for a more scientific text? But big cats have a universal appeal that cuts across generations, and I can think of nowhere easier to film them than the Masai Mara. Not only are the lions, leopards and

Every cheetah can be distinguished by the rings and spots on its tail and its individual coat markings. Amber also had a distinctive nick out of her right ear.

cheetahs extremely habituated to vehicles, making them easy to approach, but the mix of open grassy plains and acacia woodlands provides excellent visibility in which to find them. It is the perfect filming location.

One thing was certain, without the continued support of *Animal Planet*, our American co-producers, who provide a sizeable part of the budget, the series would not be recommissioned. But the feedback from American audiences was as enthusiastic as elsewhere, prompting *Animal Planet* to go for a third series. So, early in September 2000, the *Big Cat Diary* team once again gathered at a private tented camp along the banks of the Mara River just a few kilometres north of Governor's Camp. This time, though, things were to be very different.

The Mara usually receives some rain in even the bleakest of dry seasons, but not this year. We barely recognized the location of the previous series. On that occasion our tented camp had been hit by a ferocious gale, dumping one of our soundmen's tents into the middle of the river – clothes, books, mobile phone, the lot. But now

Amber would regularly jump up onto the bonnet of cars for an unimpeded view across the plains.

An adult hippo intimidating a young male who had encroached on his bend of the river. Bull hippos sometimes kill each other in territorial disputes, inflicting gaping wounds with their awesome canine tusks and peg-like lower incisors.

Kenya was suffering its third year of drought. What a transformation! Nomadic pastoralists throughout the country had lost tens of thousands of head of cattle by the time we started filming. Dust devils ripped across the plains, sucking the earth from the parched land. The pastoralists had no option but to encroach into game reserves and national parks – even private ranchland – in their search for food and water, inevitably bringing them into conflict with park authorities and landowners. Politicians pleaded with game managers to exercise tolerance during the people's time of need. At night we could hear the sounds of cowbells tinkling deep within the reserve as the Masai herded their cattle into the sanctuary. And each morning vultures filled the ashen sky, wheeling overhead, as others plummeted to the ground to feast on yet another carcass.

Ironically the drought made for spectacular filming, as all the predators were assured of plenty of food. Added to this, dry years are always the best ones to view the migration of wildebeest and zebras. As the dry easterly winds whip across the southern Serengeti at the end of the rainy season in late May and early June, the wildebeest nation turns its back on the stinging wind and moves rapidly to the north and west. The dryer the year the greater the spectacle, with the animals leaving the plains en masse. The Mara is situated in the highest rainfall area in the ecosystem, offering water and grazing during the long dry season that lasts until the onset of the short rains in mid-October. This is as far north as the herds travel – beyond lies settlement, agriculture, fences all the way to the shores of Lake Victoria. As the rains replenish the Serengeti grasslands and fill the muddy

alkaline pools with water in October and November, the wildebeest head south again to their ancestral calving grounds on the short-grass plains.

In times of drought more than half a million wildebeest flood into the Mara at the beginning of the dry season. Some of the bulls are in the first flush of the annual rut, and from the air the wildebeest look like an army of ants, the females clustered into dense knots around the territorial males, with large herds of bachelors loitering on the fringes, peacefully feeding. It is for this reason that we always choose the middle of the dry season – the months of September and October – to film *Big Cat Diary*, relying on the wildebeest and zebras – and fires – to knock down the long grass and make it easier for us to find predators.

The migration is all-pervasive. Within days the grass is gone, forcing the elephants to seek out the acacia woodlands to the north of the reserve where Half-Tail and Zawadi can be found. The presence of the migration helps to guarantee plenty of action, particularly at favoured river-crossing sites, to which the herds return year after year, gathering in their thousands to cross the river to find better grazing. The wildebeest and zebras – sometimes even the Thomson's gazelles – must brave the giant crocodiles that pilot up and down the river in search of prey. And if they survive the crocodiles there is always the threat posed by prides of lions lying in ambush or the occasional leopard that sneaks out of the thickets to snatch a wildebeest calf or zebra foal as it struggles to clamber up the riverbank. Year after year, Angie and I make our annual pilgrimage to the Mara River. No matter how many times we have witnessed the spectacle before, the noise, dust and mayhem are irresistible.

The Topi Plains males who took over the Marsh Pride territory in 2000.

While filming the first series of *Big Cat Diary* we struggled to deliver exciting footage of the Marsh Lions. The pride mostly killed at night, and for much of our stay there were no cubs to entertain us during the daytime, or they were too young to film, tucked away in the croton thickets along the Bila Shaka Lugga, the intermittent watercourse at the heart of the pride's territory. Two years later we had better luck, with a large crèche of cubs, but everything changed in late 1999 when Scruffy, one of the two pride males, and two of the five lionesses were killed by Masai pastoralists. Scruffy's death precipitated a take-over of the pride territory by two blond-maned males from the neighbouring Topi Plains Pride to the east. The Topi Plains males were quick to exploit the weakness, terrorizing Scruffy's companion Scar, and prompting a split in the pride. Though two of the adult females stayed and eventually mated with the invaders, the eleven subadults left their birthplace along the Bila Shaka Lugga and retreated to the Marsh to escape the threat posed by these new males.

The young Marsh Lions and an older female called Bump Nose, who was the mother of three of them, spent the dry season hunting around the Marsh. Scar did his best to keep out of harm's way, somehow managing to avoid outright war with the Topi Plains males and scavenging from kills made by the younger generation. While Simon watched the Marsh Lions, I kept an eye on the Ridge Pride, who live to

Up to 600,000 wildebeest migrate from the Serengeti in Tanzania to the Masai Mara during the dry season, which begins in early June and continues through to mid-October.

the south of the Musiara area. They provided us with one of the real characters of the third series, a cub named Solo who was easy for people to identify, being the only baby in the pride.

All our worries about how we were going to find enough new material to film proved unfounded. The Marsh Lions were particularly active, partly due to the wealth of hunting opportunities Musiara Marsh offers in the dry season, but also as a consequence of having so many subadults eager to try out their fledgling hunting skills – and so many mouths to feed. Nothing was too big for the subadults and they often hunted during daylight. We filmed them attempting to ambush (with varying degrees of success) hippos, buffaloes, wildebeest, zebras and warthogs. All the young lions had to do was bury

themselves in the dense reedbeds at the heart of the Marsh and wait. Sooner or later, throngs of wildebeest and zebras would file down from the high country to the north and the rolling plains to the east, slaking their thirst at the spring-fed waters. And with the hippos and buffaloes very prone to the ravages of drought – and outnumbered by the massed feeding herds of wildebeest – there were many times when these heavyweights found themselves in a life-or-death struggle with the lions.

There was plenty of action with the cheetahs, too, even though Amber's three cubs – a female and two males – had left their mother shortly after we finished filming the second series, and were fully grown. Though they were now wandering widely together, Angie and I occasionally found the two young males. They seemed

strangely wary of vehicles, unlike their sister Kike (Swahili for 'young female') who had lost none of her tameness and still regularly climbed onto vehicles. Simon spent much of his time following Amber, who was by now the oldest female in the area. He also tracked the movements of an adult male known as Nick, due to the prominent nick in his ear, the current territory-holder on the Musiara side of the river.

Kike had settled in an area to the south-east of Musiara Marsh and could often be found hunting around the eastern edge of Rhino Ridge and the plains surrounding Mara Intrepids tented camp. Simon and cameraman Warren Samuels filmed some wonderful footage of a violent spat between Kike and Nick that left the larger male with blood dripping from his nose. Such

Half-Tail disappeared in early 1999. This was the last occasion that I saw her – accompanied by her sixth litter of cubs.

aggressive encounters between widely dispersed individuals often have the desired effect and within a day or so prompt the female to come into season.

Leopards were an entirely different story. In 1999 an event of major significance had left Angie and me feeling utterly desolate and prompted us to return to the Mara during September to film a brief up-date. Earlier in the year Half-Tail had disappeared. We had followed the life of this charismatic cat since she first emerged along Fig Tree Ridge and Leopard Gorge in 1990, and as I said she had been a star of the first series of *Big Cat Diary*. By the time we filmed the second, her daughter Zawadi was fully independent, and at two and a half years old would soon mate and give birth to her first cubs. Half-Tail was nursing her sixth litter at the time and had moved further north, burying herself in an area of acacia woodlands and rocky tree-spotted hills closer to the Mara River. I remember thinking on the occasions we found her that she had finally started to show signs of age. She was now eleven, old by Mara leopard standards. Even so we managed to capture some wonderful footage of her and her two cubs. Meanwhile, Zawadi regularly entertained us with her playful antics, proving to be just as much of a character as her mother.

The events leading to Half-Tail's death remain something of a mystery. It is said that she was caught up in a wire snare set by herdsmen as she crawled through a hole in the thornbush stockade enclosing a temporary cattle boma. Apparently she had taken a goat or a sheep the previous night, and paid the price for her persistence. It was a sad end for a unique creature who had given pleasure to millions of viewers. But a leopard can be a real menace to stockmen, a murdering thief to their way of thinking, a silent hunter that visits in the dead of night.

Despite Half-Tail's absence, we found plenty to film when we returned for series three in 2000. As we had expected, Zawadi

Zawadi with her daughter Safi, aged three months. Zawadi is snarling at a hyena that she has seen approaching her along Fig Tree Ridge.

had given birth in Leopard Gorge shortly after we filmed the update in September 1999. But the two cubs lived for barely two weeks, tracked down and eaten by hyenas. Then as the sun rose on the morning of 1 January 2000 Angie, our son David and I could hardly believe our good fortune as we sat and watched Zawadi carry a half-eaten impala carcass back to where she had hidden her second litter – a male and female – along Fig Tree Ridge. It is tough raising leopard cubs in the Mara with so many lions and hyenas to compete with: within six months lions managed to kill the more adventurous male cub. Nevertheless, Zawadi and Safi, as we named her daughter – it's a Swahili term

of approval meaning a combination of 'clean' and 'nice' – provided us with many wonderful moments, spending much of their time to the north of Leopard Gorge in the area that Half-Tail used to roam.

When it was decided to film a fourth series of *Big Cat Diary* in 2002 I wondered how on earth we could compete with the kind of scenes we had filmed two years earlier. Droughts of that magnitude come along only once every five to ten years, and with people now talking about the possibility of an El Niño, I had visions of it being really wet. I imagined acres of long grass greeting us at the end of the rainy season, which in turn was likely to yield a dismal migration – and very tough times trying to find the cats. Fortunately I was wrong. What made the fourth series different was cubs – lots of them. All three big cats had youngsters for us to film – something that had been missing from the earlier series.

Angie and I travelled down to the Mara a few days before the crew assembled to catch up with what had been happening. Angie had already been networking with our friends at the various camps and lodges, who had provided us with almost daily updates on the movements of the Marsh Lions and Zawadi, who was by now heavily pregnant again. Bump Nose, one of the five original Marsh lionesses, had disappeared, leaving just two of the older generation, Khali and Notch. Meanwhile, Red – one of the Marsh Sisters, a small group of lionesses exiled from the Marsh Pride some years earlier – had been speared by the Masai after she killed a calf, leaving her companions Gimpy and Go-Kat to fend for themselves. Fortunately the Marsh Pride itself had a new generation of seven young females to bolster their number – the subadults who had featured so prominently in series three.

A few weeks before we arrived in the Mara, Angie received a report from Governor's Camp that a cheetah had given birth to five cubs along the Bila Shaka Lugga. This is the traditional birthplace of the Marsh Lions' cubs and one of the few places out on the plains where the lions can still find shade in the heat of the day. In the past whenever a cheetah has tried to raise a litter in the vicinity she has failed. Sooner or later one or more of the lions happens to look up and see her, recognizing by her behaviour that she has cubs and immediately moving in to investigate. If the cubs are small they are doomed, and so it proved in this instance. We were told that one of the Marsh Lions' new pride males was the culprit and that the cheetah mother was Amber's daughter, Kike. We had hoped that for the first time on *Big Cat Diary* we would be able to feature a cheetah with small cubs. But it would not be Kike.

In recent years cheetah numbers have plummeted in the northern Mara, especially beyond the reserve boundary. A few years ago, driving through this area early in the morning was guaranteed to yield at least one cheetah, often several. With plenty of gazelles and impalas – and fewer lions and hyenas than within the reserve – it was ideal cheetah country, and the sight of a cheetah hunting, often in the company of up to five fluff-ball cubs, was the highlight of any game drive. In those days there were more than 60 adult cheetahs living in and around the Mara, and we always assumed that those outside the reserve thrived here due to the presence of the Masai, who provided a powerful deterrent to lions and hyenas, the cheetah's main competitors. With these larger predators seeking the safety of cover during the daytime, the cheetahs could hunt and move about with their cubs in relative safety. Cheetahs are timid cats and no threat to the Masai, rarely

Warriors (*Ilmurran*) of the Kisongo Masai in northern Tanzania dancing in celebration at becoming junior elders during the colourful ceremony called *Eunoto*.

Notch (left) and her sister Khali, part of the original group of five Marsh lionesses we filmed in 1996. Notch is acting submissively as she greets her sister, who is nursing young cubs.

attempting to take livestock, and the fact that they do not scavenge renders them immune to the effects of the poison that the herdsmen sometimes employ to rid the area of predators, lacing a carcass with toxic cattle-dip.

Today the Masai are more sedentary and more numerous, bringing ever greater numbers of cattle, sheep and goats into the area surrounding the Mara Reserve. The grass is cropped short year round, leaving little cover for cheetahs to den or to provide camouflage for newly emerging cubs.

The plains around Aitong and the wooded thickets to the north of Leopard Gorge were traditionally Amber's hunting grounds. Nobody was sure how old she was, though some people thought she might be as much as 12 – almost unimaginably old by wild cheetah standards. This time when we asked after her, the drivers said that they had lost track of her in recent months and thought she had probably died. It is impossible not to feel sad when an old friend – which these cats are to us – dies or is injured. Just like Half-Tail, Amber was a huge part of our

lives: it was always so good to seek either of them out and to spend time in their company. Both cats were such distinctive characters that at first we couldn't quite believe they had gone. Even though Amber ranged widely from Paradise Plain in the south all the way to the Aitong Plains in the north-east, sooner or later she would reappear, in the same way that Half-Tail would vanish for months at a time during the long rains, submerging herself in a shroud of long red-oat grass. Then one day we would find her again, lying among the lichen-covered rocks in Leopard Gorge or feasting on a kill in a sausage tree on top of Observation Hill. But though we searched for Amber in all her old haunts there was no sign of her, and we were forced to accept that she had gone for good.

So for the first time on *Big Cat Diary*, Simon and his camera crew crossed the Mara River to search for cheetahs in that part of the reserve situated on the west of the river – the Mara Triangle. Angie and I love the Triangle; scenically it is stunning country. We were married there in 1992, on a high bluff on top of the Siria Escarpment, overlooking the Mara River. The escarpment

forms the western boundary of the reserve, one side of the 520 km² (200 sq. mile) triangle of land enclosed by the river to the east and the Kenya–Tanzania border to the south, which separates the Masai Mara from the vast Serengeti National Park. In 1995 control of the reserve was divided between the Narok County Council to the east of the river and Trans-Mara County Council to the west. A management company known as the Mara Conservancy is now responsible for running the Triangle on behalf of the Trans-Mara County Council and has made a welcome and positive impact on road maintenance, visitor surveillance and revenue collection. Since the Mara Conservancy took over more than 1,000 wire snares have been recovered and nearly 200 people arrested, sending a clear warning to meat hunters that the Triangle is no longer poachers' country.

From the first day they set foot in the Triangle, Simon and his crew were in cheetah paradise. They quickly discovered two females, each with three cubs, as well as a male, all hunting within a few kilometres of each other, barely half an hour's drive from Little Governor's Camp,

Balanites woodland is a feature of the Mara Triangle, where cheetahs are thriving, partly because there are fewer lions and hyenas.

as part of a crèche and mothers of young born within a few weeks of each other bring their cubs together as soon as they are old enough to emerge from the dense cover of their hiding place.

This was an exciting time in the history of the Marsh Lions. Angie and I were fascinated to see the way in which the young females from the group of eleven subadults who had retreated to the Marsh two years earlier had returned to the Bila Shaka Lugga as adults and mated with the new Marsh males from the Topi Plains. As sleek young four-year-olds, their lives had come full circle; they were back where they had been born, raising their own cubs.

Now they were faced with a different problem. The Marsh Pride's territory has always supported a finite number of lions, and in all the time we have watched them the pride has averaged between four and six lionesses. With the two oldest, Notch and Khali, now joined by six younger female relatives, and with ten young cubs to feed as well as the two pride males, it seemed inevitable that there would not be enough food for the whole pride once the migration deserted the Marsh for the Serengeti, unless they took to hunting buffaloes. I suspect that when we return for the next series, much will have changed in the Musiara area.

where the film cars were stationed overnight. Simon concentrated on the female with the younger cubs, which were about three months old when filming commenced. He called the female Honey. Sometimes the two cheetah mothers were within sight of each other, though typically these solitary cats kept their distance and simply avoided each other rather than needlessly fighting over turf. There were nail-biting confrontations with lions, and as filming came to a close Simon and the cheetah crew managed to film a dramatic encounter between Honey and her cubs and the territorial male.

Meanwhile on the other side of the river, a new presenter, Saba Douglas-Hamilton, joined us to watch over the Marsh Lions. At first we thought this would be a relatively easy assignment for Saba, but things soon got complicated with three of the lionesses giving birth to cubs within weeks of each other along the Bila Shaka Lugga, while other members of the pride concentrated

their activity around the Marsh. It is quite normal for lionesses in the same pride to come into season at the same time, particularly after a takeover, when any young cubs sired by the previous males are invariably killed by the newcomers. The best way for lionesses to raise their cubs is

The 1,500 elephants living in and around the Masai Mara are a potent force for change in the landscape, contributing to the present shift from woodland to grassland.

The biggest surprise during the last series was finding Solo, the lion cub who had kept us enthralled with his antics throughout series three. Solo was the only survivor of a litter of four born to the oldest lioness in the Ridge Pride. He was full of character, a tough little cub whose only playmates were many months older than he was. I felt sure that, come the rainy season, Solo would find it impossible to compete with all those hungry mouths (there were more than 20 lions in the Ridge Pride) and would be bullied out of his share at any kills. But I obviously hadn't taken into account Solo's tenacious character. He had been raised in the white-hot cauldron of competition where no quarter is sought or given. The two magnificent old pride males had long since been chased from the pride and were probably dead by now, but there was Solo, bossing around his older relatives as if he owned the place.

Solo's mother had died since the last series, and three of the other adult females were heavily pregnant, possibly due to the arrival of two four-year-old males who had appeared with the migration and may have come from the Serengeti. This group was tentatively forming a new pride, though the males and females were rarely seen together. The rest of the pride roamed around the fringes of the riverine forest to the south of Governor's Camp without males to protect them, doing their best to avoid conflict with the Marsh Pride, who were numerically far stronger. The Ridge Pride now consisted of four young males of just over three years of age, and their two sisters – Solo's one-time playmates. Accompanying them was an old female whom we named Gimpy, a brave, defiant old lioness who aggressively defended her younger relatives – hence the damaged front leg that earned her her name.

Sharing the same area and wandering even further afield were Solo and his three-year-old male companion, the youngest of the older generation of cubs. These two itinerant males had formed a strong bond

Young male lions become nomadic when they are two to three years old, and must compete with the more numerous hyenas for food.

that would continue throughout their lives – if they survived the next two years as nomads. They were in endless conflict with their older relatives, disputing kills and scrapping over living space. It was a stark reminder of just how tough life can be for lions during this transitional time. Many never make it. Lacking a territory of their own, Solo and his chum were forced to keep on the move. As long as the wildebeest remained in the area, providing easy pickings for all the predators, they could find enough to eat, though it often meant warring with members of the local hyena clans, who were always ready to dispute ownership of a kill with young lions such as these.

Who knows where Solo will be in two years' time? By then he will be in the first flush of adulthood, and if he and his companion survive they will be ready to stake their claim to a pride territory somewhere in the Mara–Serengeti.

Events such as I have described are the daily fare of game drives in the Masai Mara, which over time have provided us with an insight into the lives of the most charismatic animals. There is always something new or interesting to discover, and I never tire of watching lions hunting or playing – or even just lying there doing nothing at all. I have always maintained that my favourite creature is the one that Angie and I happen to be following at the time – be it wild dogs, lions or leopards. But there is something special about leopards which sets them apart and which I hope will become apparent in the pages of this book. This story is not only about the African leopard, nor just about the particular leopards that Angie and I have come to know over the years – Chui, the Mara Buffalo female, Half-Tail and Zawadi. It is an attempt – as was *Big Cat Diary: Lion* (the first book in this series of three) – to look at Africa's big cats from a broader perspective. We examine the findings of the latest field research and conservation initiatives, which in the case of the leopard stretch far beyond the African continent. The leopard is the world's most adaptable and widespread large cat. Long may it remain so.

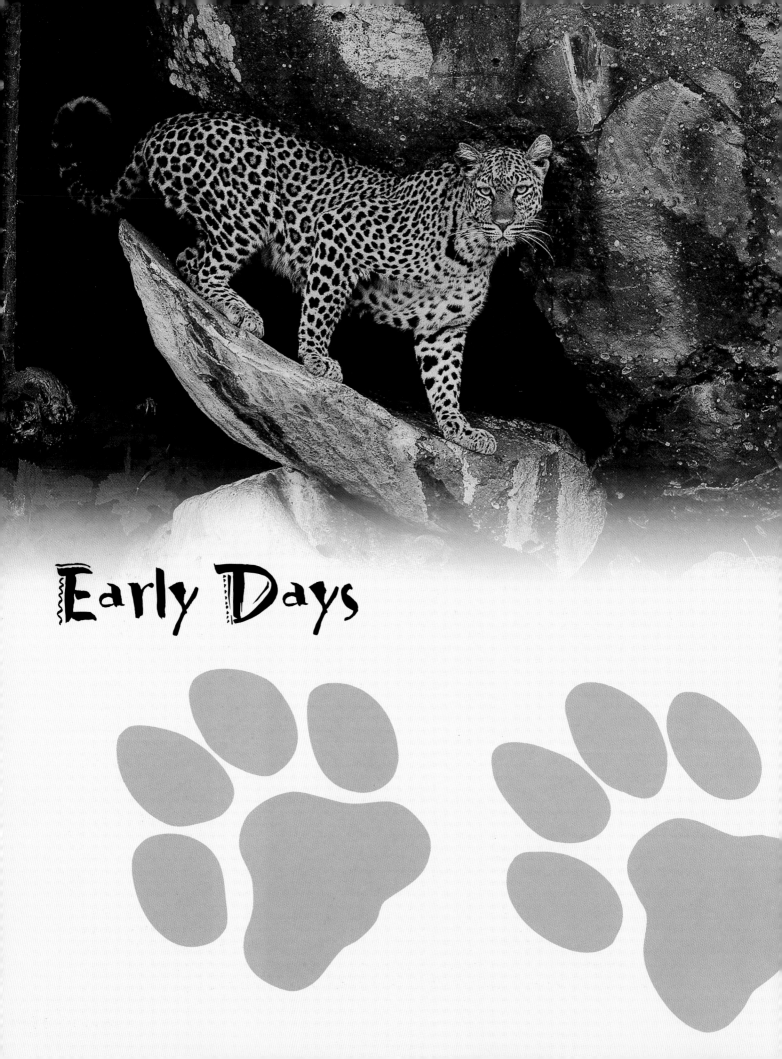

Early Days

Chui with a young impala. Impalas are a favourite prey of leopards wherever the two species occur together.

'Even before I first set foot in Africa ten years ago, I knew which of the wild animals I most wanted to see. It was the leopard that embodied my idea of Africa: an animal of supreme grace and agility, a hunter of the dark concealed in a spotted coat.

When I was a small child on a Berkshire farm, the annual visit to Regent's Park Zoo was the highlight of my year. I still remember standing spellbound in front of a barren enclosure as a huge male leopard padded up and down. Occasionally it would pause and stare at me through pale green eyes before setting off again on its endless journey. Surely this must be "the cat that walked by himself", I thought, equally convinced that Rudyard Kipling really did know the secret of "How the Leopard got his spots". But I knew if I wanted to learn more about leopards then I would have to journey to Africa.'

I wrote those words 20 years ago in the introduction to my book *The Leopard's Tale*. It had taken me six years of living in the Masai Mara to complete the book: that was how difficult it was in the 1970s to find a leopard that you could watch, let alone photograph.

I first visited the Mara in 1974 on a four-month overland trip from London to Johannesburg. In those days the Mara was little more than a stopover en route to the great Serengeti National Park in Tanzania or on the way back to Nairobi. There was time for only a single game drive, but that was enough. I knew even then that I wanted to return – the Mara is a predator's paradise.

When I arrived in South Africa at the end of my trip, I happened to pick up a copy of the *Rand Daily Mail*. It was one of those defining moments, a stroke of luck that helped determine that I stay on in Africa, rather than continuing my travels by boat from Cape Town to Sydney in Australia. An article by Dr Theodore Bailey had caught my eye. Bailey had just begun his study of leopards in the Kruger National Park, a massive tract of wooded savanna in the Transvaal Lowveld that stretches along

South Africa's eastern boundary, bordering Mozambique. The Kruger is 320 km (200 miles) from north to south and 65 km (40 miles) from east to west at its widest, an area of 19,485 km^2 (7,800 sq. miles). At the time it received 360,000 tourists annually.

The article was accompanied by pictures of Bailey tracking his study animals using radio-telemetry, a technique that was in its infancy. Here was somebody doing what I wanted to do, spending their time in the bush watching big cats. I immediately wrote to Bailey and asked him if he needed an assistant. He didn't. His wife was able to offer whatever support he needed, and besides if I was serious about studying predators I should continue my studies at university as a postgraduate student (I had told him I had a first degree in zoology). I appreciated the fact that he replied at all – I imagine he must have been inundated with requests such as mine.

Following Bailey's advice I then applied to the Pretoria Mammal Research Institute, who generously offered me the chance to study predators in Zimbabwe for my Masters degree. But I felt uncomfortable accepting the offer when the majority of South Africans were still disenfranchised by the apartheid system. That was the closest I ever came to becoming a scientist. The only options left to me if I wanted to work with wildlife were to become a safari guide, or to

develop my interest in wildlife art. Apart from the article on the leopard project, the *Rand Daily Mail* had other reasons to inspire me. The newspaper was running a series of articles about wildlife written by Sue Hart, a veterinary surgeon who once helped George Adamson patch up one of his beloved lions and who writes with poetic passion about wild Africa. But it was the beautiful stippled pen-and-ink sketches by Lee Voight that caught my attention. I had always loved to draw and had dabbled with pointillism (or stippling) at university to illustrate my honours thesis. The detail and range of tones that you can produce with a graphic pen are outstanding. Hart and Voight had published a collection of their work in book form, which I duly rushed out and bought – along with a set of Rotring pens and reams of art paper.

For the next two years I managed to find temporary work in Botswana with various wildlife-related projects, before heading back to Kenya to make the Mara my home. I based myself at Mara River Camp, which in those days was owned by legendary paleontologist Richard Leakey and wildlife filmmaker Alan Root. The deal was that I received free board and lodging in return for keeping an eye on the camp and acting as the in-house naturalist. This would allow me the chance to explore the Mara while taking guests on game drives; at the same

Leopards are secretive creatures, preferring to remain hidden among thickets and rocky outcrops to avoid being detecting by potential prey or by other predators.

time I could develop my interest in animal behaviour and wildlife illustration. By then my first set of pen-and-ink drawings had been published as prints, and within a couple of years I had earned enough from my art work to buy a Toyota Landcruiser. This brought me the freedom at last to go out on my own and get serious about my new passion – wildlife photography.

Though I had abandoned any ideas I might have had of continuing my studies as a zoologist, my academic training never left me. To this day, I still meticulously record whatever I see when I am in the bush. I have a pile of notebooks in my study in Nairobi filled with drawings and details of the animals I encountered, dating back to the time when I first arrived in the Mara.

Big cats have always featured prominently in these journals. There were plenty of lions for me to watch. Cheetahs too were relatively easy to track down in those days, and there was one female with three large cubs who treated vehicles just as Amber and her offspring would do years later – jumping onto spare wheels, clambering over roof hatches and generally enjoying themselves. It was unusual to come back from a game drive without having seen at least one of these elegant cats. Leopards were quite another matter. Neither lions nor cheetahs make a point of hiding themselves away, often appearing in open country and easy to approach. My failure to find a leopard just heightened my appetite for discovering all that I could about the most elusive of Africa's big cats.

I had seen my first leopard in the Serengeti during the overland trip, a glorious male shrouded in golden grass resting at the base of a yellow-barked acacia tree. We waited for him to rouse himself and climb back up into the tree to feast on the half-eaten impala that he had stored safely out of reach of lions and hyenas, 6m (20ft) up in the air. But leopards have a different sense of time from humans. This one was in no hurry to provide us with a better view of his spotted coat.

After I settled in the Mara I was not to see a leopard for many months, even though I was now living in some of the best leopard country in Africa. The problem, of course, was that stunningly beautiful coat. Concerns for the plight of spotted cats worldwide were first voiced in the 1960s, leading to various countries imposing voluntary bans on the trade in leopard skins. In 1972 the United States classified the leopard as an endangered species throughout its entire range, and the International Union for the Conservation of Nature (IUCN) listed five subspecies of leopards as rare or endangered. A report by Norman Myers published in 1974 on the status of leopards and cheetahs for the IUCN and World Wildlife Fund estimated that during the 1960s as many as 50,000 leopards were being killed each year in Africa to supply the seemingly endless demand for fur coats. In 1968 and 1969 alone fur brokers in the United States imported the skins of more than 17,000 leopards, and in 1980 Europe imported nearly half a million skins of medium-sized and small cats such as clouded leopards

Though food, water and cover are the basic requirements of life for most species, leopards are so adaptable that they can live virtually anywhere. They have the widest distribution of any cat, ranging far beyond the African continent. Leopards are still found in parts of Israel, the Near and Middle East, Iran, Pakistan, India, much of South-East Asia and the Malaysian archipelago, north over the Himalayas through Tibet, southern China and into Siberia. The pattern of spots and rosettes on their coats mimics the dapple of leafy shade, a geometric abstraction that helps to mirror the background, merging the leopard with its surroundings. Even a scarcity of cover can be overcome – the leopard simply confines itself to the hours of darkness. It has proved itself a master of living close to human habitation, something that is impossible for lions or cheetahs.

Leopards can go without drinking water for long periods, remaining primarily nocturnal in very dry areas.

and ocelots. Thankfully many countries are now members of the Convention on International Trade in Endangered Species (CITES), which banned the sale of leopard skins in 1975. Some of the smaller species have not been so fortunate.

Big cats in areas such as the Mara and Serengeti – national game reserves and parks – had already enjoyed protection from all forms of hunting for many years by the time these figures were published. In fact the 1960s had seen the dawning of a new awareness about the way wild animals lived and behaved, and leading conservationists such as Professor Bernhard Grzimek (author of *Serengeti Shall Not Die*, which became not only a successful book but also an Oscar-winning film) had encouraged tourism to parks and reserves as a way of helping to pay for conservation and promoting concern for the fate of wildlife. Gradually the word safari began to take on a new meaning. Visitors now came armed with cameras rather than guns. It

didn't take long for the wild animals to become habituated to people in vehicles, and places such as the tree-lined Seronera Valley in Serengeti were famous the world over as *the* place to see leopards. Tour leaders and drivers could pretty much guarantee that at some point on your safari they would be able to show you a leopard. I remember admiring a photograph of a magnificent male whose territory overlapped parts of the Seronera Valley, standing profiled in a fever tree. The guides named him 'Good as Gold', as a tribute to his co-operative nature.

That all changed as the demand for skins increased and the price that traders were willing to pay for a leopard skin skyrocketed. Visitors to Governor's Camp in the Masai Mara suddenly found that the handful of leopards who could be approached at close quarters had vanished; so too did Good as Gold. It wasn't just the skin trade. Prior to the ban on trophy-hunting in Kenya in early 1977, leopards

Zawadi with a Thomson's gazelle kill – another of the leopard's favourite prey.

were being baited and killed illegally in and around the reserve. By the time I arrived at Mara River Camp in 1977, it was impossible to find a leopard who would tolerate close observation, and during my first year there I saw a leopard on only two occasions – fleeting glimpses of a spotted coat melting away among the acacia thickets.

But leopards are adaptable creatures. Given the chance they will bounce back and repopulate an area, particularly if lion and hyena numbers are low, and provided they are left in peace by man – their greatest enemy. In time I was able to unravel some of the mysteries of how these beautiful creatures live in the wild.

Leopards are most commonly associated with some type of forest cover from tropical rainforests to savanna woodlands, and inhabit rocky hills and mountainous terrain up to elevations of 5,000m (16,250ft) or more. They reach their highest densities in forested regions, and in parts of West Africa and tropical Asia they live in forests where the mean annual rainfall is well over 2,000mm (80in). Temperature does not seem to be a major influence on distribution: leopards are capable of moulding their behaviour to the blistering heat of semi-arid areas as easily as to the bitter winters of colder regions. Though they do not occur in true deserts such as

the Sahara, they can live in areas with virtually no rainfall, going for long periods without drinking. But cats have very few sweat glands and rely on panting to help regulate their body temperature. In dry habitats such as the Kalahari in southern Africa, leopards are active only during the cooler hours and do most of their hunting at night so as not to overstress themselves, relying on the blood and body fluids of their prey to meet their moisture requirements, and at times eating fruit such as tsama melons and wild cucumbers.

As if to prove the point about their adaptability, the frozen remains of a leopard lie entombed near the summit of Mount Kilimanjaro, some 5,800m (19,000ft) above the African plains, and in China and Russia leopards at times endure subfreezing temperatures, growing a thicker coat to counteract the cold. But they are not as well adapted to snowy climes as their relative the snow leopard, which has thick cushions of fur between its pads to insulate its feet in winter and to help spread its weight like a snowshoe.

The leopard's adaptability to a wide variety of habitats goes hand in hand with its catholic taste in food – 92 prey species are recorded in sub-Saharan Africa. Nothing is too small for a hungry leopard, and they will take insects such as dung beetles, reptiles, birds' eggs and nestlings, as well as small mammals and carrion – even humans – though those living in game-rich sanctuaries such as the Mara–Serengeti gain most of their sustenance from impalas or gazelles. There is even a record of a leopard killing a full-grown male eland – Africa's largest antelope, which can weigh up to 900kg (1,980lb). The leopard is the cat for all seasons.

Despite its adaptability, there is no doubt that the leopard's distribution and numbers have diminished in recent times. Fossils dating back to 1.5–2 million years ago (mya) hint at a greater range – leopard remains have been found in Pleistocene deposits in Europe, the Middle East, India,

Male leopards are immensely powerful creatures, 30–50 per cent heavier than females. Older males develop a dewlap of loose skin down the throat which often extends along the belly.

further north in Asia than today, as well as on the island of Sumatra, and of course in Africa. The leopard of those times was certainly equal in size to recent forms, and specimens from Java and Palestine were somewhat larger.

There is sufficient variation in the leopard's coat markings and colour from one region to another for some taxonomists to assign them to different subspecies. Jonathan Kingdon, in his wonderful treatise on the evolution of East African mammals, has a colourful illustration showing the skins of leopards from a variety of regions: Ethiopia, Ruwenzori, Zambia, Somalia, the Cape, Zanzibar (now thought to be extinct) and Mount Elgon in Kenya. Leopards from the Democratic Republic of the Congo are said to be consistently small and greenish in comparison to other populations, while those from Anatolia, Lebanon and Iraq are described as consistently large, tan and with markings quite distinctive from those of northern Iran. In a paper written in 1932 by Pocock, savanna leopards were described as

rufous to ochraceous; desert leopards as pale cream to yellow-brown, with those from cooler regions being more grey; rainforest leopards a dark, deep gold and high-mountain leopards even darker.

Colour variations such as these led to over 30 subspecies of leopards being described in the 1950s, but recent work using molecular biology points to only six geographically isolated groups – the African, central Asian, Indian, Sri Lankan, Javan and east Asian – and says that only eight subspecies should be recognized. The 12 African subspecies are now lumped together as *Panthera pardus pardus* (the so-called North African leopard, although its range is actually south of the Sahara from West Africa to Eritrea). The six subspecies from Central Asia are now known as *P. p. saxicolor* (the Persian leopard), the Arabian leopard as *P. p. nimr*, the Sri Lankan as *P. p. kotiya* (the top predator on the island), the Javan as *P. p. melas* (also top predator since the Javan tiger went extinct in the 1970s), the South China as *P. p. delacouri*, the North China as

P. p. japonensis and the Amur or Far Eastern leopard as *P. p. orientalis*.

Black or melanistic leopards, with coats that are so heavily pigmented that they appear black – a feature caused by a recessive gene – gave rise to considerable confusion when they were first observed and were thought to be a different species – the fabled black panther immortalized in Rudyard Kipling's stories. They are not. The rosettes can be seen patterning the dark coat in reflected light. Leopards from humid forested areas tend to have darker coats and melanistic individuals are more common in these areas and in mountainous regions. They are found more often in Asia than Africa – though a black leopard was recently seen in an area bordering the Masai Mara. In the dense forests of the Malay Peninsula, up to 50 per cent of the leopards are said to be black. This seems to follow the assumption that dark colouring in mammals occurs more frequently in warm, humid regions, though in the case of the jaguar, which also has a melanistic form, this may not be so.

Male and female leopards do not differ in any great respect, unlike the more social lions, where males have a mane and are instantly recognizable from the smaller females – when you live together it is more important to be able to distinguish males from females. Male leopards are certainly considerably bigger and more powerful than females, in some cases weighing up to 50 per cent more, and with broader heads and heavier muzzles. Both sexes have massive skulls to allow for the attachment of strong jaw muscles. Older males often develop a pronounced dewlap – a loose flap of skin under the throat, sometimes running along the stomach. But coat markings and coat colour are similar. Leopards of both sexes vary greatly in size according to area, probably because of prey availability and the fact that it is advantageous to be larger in colder conditions, in order to reduce heat loss, and in more open terrain where you are likely to be hunting larger prey. This is also the case with the jaguar – the largest individuals live in less forested habitats.

In most parts of East and Southern Africa male leopards weigh in at 60–65kg (130–145lb), with females averaging 40–45kg (88–100lb). Males of more than 70kg (150lb) in weight and 2.3m (7ft 6in) in length including the tail are considered exceptionally large. There is a photograph in Jay Mellon's book *African Hunter* that I will always remember – it shows a 93kg (205lb) male leopard shot by a client of professional hunter Tony France on the dense forested slopes of Mount Kenya. This is a huge animal almost the size of a lioness, though if it had recently gorged itself this might account for up to 20 per cent of its weight. A number of people have recorded seeing large leopards in the Aberdare Forest and Mount Kenya regions,

Half-Tail stretching before setting off to hunt. Leopards are consummate stalkers, creeping to within a few metres of their prey before rushing forward and pouncing.

perhaps because of a high density of medium-sized prey such as bushbuck, less competition from other predators – and plenty of trees in which to stash kills. Leopards from the Cape Province in South Africa are much smaller, with males averaging just over 30kg (65lb) and females around 20kg (45lb) – an adaptation no doubt to their prey, which is limited to smaller fare such as rock hyrax and the occasional klipspringer.

Of the five big cats lumped together in the genus *Panthera*, and sometimes referred to as roaring cats, the leopard and the somewhat larger and stockier jaguar are the most similar in appearance, and both produce a cough-like roar. Though the African leopard generally has smaller, more numerous rosettes than the jaguar and normally lacks spots within the rosettes, some Asian leopards have larger rosettes, superficially similar to those of the jaguar, making it difficult to distinguish one skin from another at times. Though the leopard's skull is similar to the tiger's, the skeleton is more like the jaguar's, with relatively short legs better suited to tree-climbing, and it is likely that the leopard and jaguar are the most closely related of the pantherine cats. The fact that young lions show a similar pattern of rosettes to the leopard and jaguar, which may even be present along the margins of the belly and upper legs in adult lions, together with the ability to utter a structured series of roars, or 'roaring

proper', not found in the tiger or snow leopard (which some people argue should not be included in *Panthera* – it does not roar, among other things) hints at a close relationship for all three cats. In all probability the ancestor of the lion was a spotted cat that lived in more densely forested habitat.

Though the early history of the genus *Panthera* is not well known, the work of molecular biologists such as Stephen O'Brien and his co-workers supports the idea that the pantherine cats evolved into distinct species more recently than other groups, probably within the last two million years. But at present the fossil evidence does not support this. Attempts to clarify the evolution and classification of cats have been the subject of long and bitter debate, though most taxonomists now agree that there are 36 species (at most 39).

One of the biggest stumbling blocks to sorting out the relationship between the species has been the very nature of cats. Though varying in size, coat pattern, colouring and social behaviour, cats are strikingly similar in shape and design, from the mighty tiger to the pint-sized domestic cat. All cats stalk, chase and then pounce on their prey (though as a coursing predator the cheetah might be considered an exception to this). The anatomy of the skull with its short face and binocular vision, the long stabbing canines, scissor-like carnassials and feet armed with retractable claws are

Serval cats, distinguished by their large ears and short tails, favour long-grass areas and marshland. They locate their prey primarily by hearing and then pounce on it, holding it down with their forepaws and killing it with a bite to the neck or head.

The older of the Topi Plains males returning to cover early one morning. Male lions are warriors and will fight to defend their territory against other coalitions of males. Most die a violent death, killed by other lions or hyenas, wounded by buffaloes, shot by trophy-hunters or killed by livestock-owners when they attempt to take cattle.

similar throughout the family, reflecting the supple build of the specialist hunter.

Cats in all their varied forms are grouped into a single family called the Felidae. The so-called 'true cats', those with conical canines, belong to the subfamilies Felinae and Pantherinae, while the sabre-toothed cats with their flattened and elongated upper canines are grouped in the subfamily Machairodontinae. The Felinae include Africa's smallest cat, the black-footed cat, weighing just 1.5–2.5kg (3–5lb), as well as the mountain lion or cougar with males weighing up to 100kg (220lb), while the Pantherinae include the various species of lynx (of which the caracal is one), as well the largest of all cats such as the lion and tiger. Being large predators they reside at the top of the food chain, and for this reason are far scarcer than their prey: in

order to survive, any animal must be outnumbered or outweighed by its food source. This is one of the reasons that cats are poorly represented in the fossil record – antelopes and zebras will always outnumber the predators that feed on them.

The first of the modern or true cats is thought to have been *Proailurus*, an example of which, *Proailurus lemanensis*, was found in deposits at Saint-Gerard-le-Puy, France, dating back to the Oligocene, 30 mya. *Proailurus* had more teeth than today's cats and stood about 38cm (15in) at the shoulder, half the height of a male leopard in his prime. Its skeleton suggests that it was similar in shape to the living fossa of Madagascar and, though slightly larger, was probably just as adept at climbing and jumping from branch to branch. In the New World the earliest known cat is a proailurine, found in Nebraskan Miocene deposits from around 16 mya. *Proailurus'* likely Miocene descendent was *Pseudaelurus* – a cat about the size of a large lynx – which emerged about 20 mya. *Pseudaelurus* is thought to be ancestral to the modern, living and fossil conical-toothed species of true cats, and to the now extinct sabre-toothed species known as machairodonts. Most of the known felids are confined to the past 10 million years, though we lack any clear idea of the immediate ancestry of the living species or the precise pattern of relationships between them.

Species that have been separated for a long time show a greater divergence in their DNA, and on this basis Stephen O'Brien and his colleagues initially divided the cat family into three distinct lineages. Around 12 mya the seven species of small South American cats such as the margay and ocelot branched off, followed 8–10 mya by the wild cat lineage (from which the domestic cat evolved), numbering six species. Finally, 4–6 mya the *Panthera* lineage branched off. Its 24 species include members of both the subfamilies Felinae and Pantherinae. This group boasts an array

of medium-sized and large cats, together with members of the genus *Panthera* – the lion, tiger, leopard and jaguar, commonly referred to as the big cats – as well as two fossil species, *Panthera gombaszoegensis* (the European jaguar) and *P. shaubi* (a cat the size of a small leopard or very large lynx). The most recent development in this group occurred 1.8–3.8 mya, leading to a

More than 200,000 zebras migrate through the Mara–Serengeti ecosystem, often arriving first in the long-grass areas at the end of the rainy season. They have a potentially lethal kick and can crush a lion's skull or break its jaw.

split between the lynxes and the large cats of the genus *Panthera*.

That was the state of our knowledge until ten years ago. But the latest information brought together in Mel and Fiona Sunquist's outstanding reference work *Wild Cats of the World* points to eight major cat lineages rather than three. The domestic cat lineage and that of the small cats of South America remain the same, while the *Panthera* lineage has undergone further revision and now comprises just six species: jaguar, tiger, lion, leopard, snow leopard and clouded leopard. Of these, the clouded leopard was the first to diverge from the ancestral line, followed by the snow leopard, with the lion, tiger, jaguar and leopard diverging more recently, 2–3 mya. The remaining 18 species are reclassified into a further five major lineages, with the origins of the serval, marbled cat, rusty-spotted cat and manui something of a mystery. The puma and closely related jaguarundi are grouped with the cheetah. Fossil evidence proves that cheetahs occurred in North America as far back as 2–3 mya, and they are thought to

Infant baboons begin to ride jockey-style from the age of about five weeks. The black coat they are born with gradually turns to a uniform light brown by the time they are four to six months old.

have diverged from their common ancestor 8.25 mya. The closely related leopard cat, fishing cat and flat-headed cat of South-East Asia diverged from a common ancestor only 3.95 mya, making them one of the most recent lineages. The Eurasian and Canada lynx share an older ancestor with the bobcat, and form a separate lineage with the Iberian lynx. The desert lynx or caracal and the African golden cat share a common ancestor 4.85 mya ago, sufficient to warrant their own lineage. The bay cat lineage also contains just two species, the bay cat and Asiatic golden cat, believed to have diverged from a common ancestor 4.9–5.3 mya.

It seems strange to think that there were once lions, leopards, jaguars and cheetahs in Europe, with the cheetah being the first to appear in the fossil record some 2.1 mya years ago in France. The European jaguar is recorded in Italy at around 1.6 mya ago, and it is particularly well represented in

England at the middle Pleistocene site of Westbury-sub-Mendip, just to the south of Bristol, home of the BBC Natural History Unit. It seems to have been a larger animal than the New World jaguar, *Panthera onca*. The leopard makes its first appearance in the fossil record in Europe around 0.9 mya at Vallonnet in the south of France, though the only place where it is well represented is the Italian cave site of Equi. This patchy fossil record is probably more to do with the leopard's solitary and secretive nature than with any accurate representation of its distribution and abundance.

At one time the leopard inhabited an area equivalent in size to that occupied by the tiger and lion combined, though it does not appear to have crossed into North America, where another secretive and solitary species, the mountain lion, *Puma concolor*, intermediate in size between the leopard and the jaguar, occupies the same ecological niche. The lion first appears in

Europe at Isernia in Italy, around 0.7 mya, and then becomes fairly common across most of Europe.

It has long been believed that a jaguar-like ancestor of the genus *Panthera* evolved some 2 million years ago in Eurasia and spread over Africa, Europe, southern and northern Asia and North America, later giving rise to the living species. One possibility is that the ancestral leopard then became extinct throughout the world except for Africa, with the modern leopard later spreading out of Africa again. But fossil remains of leopards and lions found at the famous archaeological site of Laetoli in Tanzania, where Mary Leakey discovered man's ancient footprints, date back 3.5 million years, pointing to an African genesis, and certainly in the lightly wooded savannas of East Africa 2 mya, the leopard would have included australopithecine hominids among its prey. John Cavalo, who studied leopards in the Serengeti in the

1980s, believes that while leopards were indeed predators of our early ancestors, the latter in turn no doubt climbed up into trees to scavenge animal flesh and marrow from the leopard's larder. Fossil evidence from South Africa attests to leopard predation on both early hominids and baboons 1–2 mya. One fossil skull of a juvenile australopithecine bears two small holes that match the lower canines of a leopard skull found in the same site.

Ancient and isolated, the African continent of around 3.2 mya provided a rich mosaic of habitats, allowing most species to survive changes in the environment. This is in sharp contrast to Europe, Asia and North America, where shifting climatic conditions had a marked effect on the native flora and fauna, leading to the extinction of many species. At some point the unknown ancestor of the larger pantherine cats evolved. It would have had both the strength and the agility to chase and overpower large agile prey like wildebeest and zebras – creatures that were too nimble for the sabre-toothed cats and too strong for the smaller pantherines. A number of modern carnivores appear at fossil sites, first in eastern and later in southern Africa, including the lion, leopard, cheetah and spotted hyena. For the next 2 million years, these species lived side by side with the old order of sabre-toothed and false sabre-toothed cats such as *Homotherium*, *Megantereon* and *Dinofelis*, during which time the forests and woodlands of eastern Africa were transformed into bush and savanna, and the Sahara Desert became a permanent feature.

For a while the sabre-toothed cats and light-heavyweight pantherines were both able to find sufficient prey to feed on. But 1.5 mya Africa's climate began to grow colder and the mega-herbivores on which the sabre-tooths had relied disappeared. As their prey dwindled and competition with man became ever more intense, these cats vanished. It was the turn of the pantherines to dominate the predator hierarchy, with large, agile cats such as the lion, which can sprint at 60kph (nearly 40mph) and weigh up to 200kg (440lb), leading the way. Gone was the dentition that had been so successful in the era of huge, thick-skinned herbivores such as the mammoth and rhino. Instead of slashing and wounding their prey with dagger-like canines, lions, leopards and cheetahs strangled their prey by clamping their jaws over its throat or, in the case of lions, by biting over the mouth and nose of large prey such as a buffalo to suffocate it. Of the modern pantherines, the clouded leopard (it is not a leopard) of South-East Asia, weighing up to 30kg (65lb) and about the size of a small leopard, is the only living cat with teeth that come anywhere near to rivalling those of the sabre-toothed cats. It has canines measuring up to 44mm (1.7in), which it uses to kill wild pigs. The clouded leopard is thought to be an evolutionary link between big and smaller cats, though little is known about these reclusive carnivores. Their climbing skills put even the agile leopard to shame; they possess ankle joints that can swivel, allowing them to climb underneath the branches of trees, hang by their hind feet and descend head first, whereas a leopard is sometimes forced to come down backwards if a tree-trunk is tall and vertical. Clouded leopards are hunted for their distinctive fur, their large teeth and even for their bones, which are believed by some to have healing powers; like many of the world's spotted cats it is threatened by man's activities.

The migratory movements of humans from Africa to Europe and then onwards around the world were mirrored by the patterns of dispersal of lions, leopards and hyenas. Early humans would have competed with these predators for food, at times scavenging from their kills. But when our genus *Homo* arose, humans began to dominate the others in a way not seen before, hunting and foraging in groups. The development of weapons to protect our puny bodies – first clubs fashioned from wood and bone, then spears and poisoned arrows, and finally guns – spelt the beginning of the end for the large predators. But the secretive leopard has survived man's onslaught better than most.

Half-Tail (before she lost her tail) carrying a male Thomson's gazelle to cover.

The Elusive Leopard

The mere mention of the word leopard inspires thoughts of a cat that remains hidden, the reluctant star of the show whose allure is only magnified by its desire to remain in the shadows. It is not by chance that the leopard wears a coat of spots and rosettes, allowing it to merge with the sunlight and shadow of the forest canopy. It is a question of survival. Leopards are designed to be invisible to enemies and prey alike. They must employ the utmost stealth to stalk within touching distance of their prey, before engaging in a short chase and a pounce, ending with their long canine teeth clamped around the victim's throat. The leopard that makes itself visible is the leopard that is shot by a trophy-hunter or killed by a poacher; the leopard that reveals its hiding place is the leopard that loses the chance of catching prey, and risks conflict with lions and hyenas. There is little that a leopard doesn't view as a potential meal, prompting alarm calls to ring out from all directions when it is on the move, warning every creature in the vicinity to be on the alert. Little wonder that leopards prefer to remain hidden for much of the time.

I can remember many years ago spotting a leopard slinking away from the base of a fig tree where it had been hurriedly trying to remove the stomach from a freshly killed impala so that it could hoist its catch to safety. I drove forward a short distance and then stopped in the hope that it might reappear, scanning the bushes with my binoculars. But hard as I tried I could not see it, until I realized that it was crouched just a metre or so from my car, buried amid a tangle of grass and thorn branches. It lay there, watchful, barely visible, pale green eyes – or were they yellow? – fixed on my vehicle, relying on the fact that I would not see it as long as it remained motionless. I carefully backed away, then sat and watched through my binoculars from a distance of 100m (330 ft) or more. Gradually the leopard relaxed, then crawled back, snake-like, to the impala and carried on plucking the fur from the carcass. I stayed there all day, forgoing breakfast and lunch, waiting to see if the leopard would succeed in treeing its kill before the sharp noses of the hyenas picked up the scent of fresh meat.

Half-Tail anxiously looking around as she tries to hide a freshly killed male impala, weighing considerably more than she does. Hyenas stole the kill before she could haul it into a tree.

Zawadi resting in one of her favourite fig trees. Not all leopards spend much time in trees, but Zawadi invariably seeks out a suitable branch to rest on in the middle of the day.

In those days nothing was more important to me than spending time with a leopard.

When Norman Myers published his report on spotted cats and the fur trade in 1974, he noted that leopards were still abundant in only five of the 40-something countries south of the Sahara, and were holding their own in 15 others. A year later, Cynthia Moss produced a book called *Portraits in the Wild: Animal Behaviour in East Africa*, a highly readable account of the findings of field biologists, giving an up-to-date picture of each species' social organization, behaviour and general ecology. This was just the book I needed now that I was acting as a driver-guide at Mara River Camp. In the section on Africa's big cats, lions warranted 28 pages, cheetahs 21 pages and leopards just 13, highlighting how little was known about leopards at that time. In fact there had not been a single scientific paper published dealing exclusively with the ecology or behaviour of free-ranging leopards in Africa. The only book that I could find devoted entirely to

leopards was Turnbull-Kemp's *The Leopard*, published in 1960, which was filled with interesting snippets on the leopard in history, hunting, man-eating and in captivity. But it contained little information on the behaviour of wild leopards – there simply wasn't any.

At that time, the Serengeti was the only park or reserve in Africa where leopards could readily be seen without the aid of baits set in artificial light. George Schaller, who studied lions in the Serengeti from 1966 to 1969, watched leopards whenever he could, but even though a number of leopards in his study area tolerated vehicles, they all too easily melted into cover when they became active, making them difficult to see or follow. It was for reasons such as this that Ted Bailey decided to employ the relatively new technique of radio-telemetry to help him track leopards on a regular basis in Kruger National Park in South Africa.

The beauty of radio-telemetry is that you can study certain aspects of the behaviour

and ecology of shy and elusive species in their natural habitat without having to see them. Bailey had been one of the pioneers of radio-telemetry in the 1960s, when it was used to track mountain lions and bobcats in Idaho in the United States, in order to document territorialism and its function in the regulation of these populations. First Bailey had to catch the leopards, using metal box-traps with a single sliding door. These had to be positioned 1–3m (3–10ft) above the ground in trees to prevent hyenas and lions from entering them. The traps were baited with portions of carcasses from annual culling operations – part of Kruger's management policy to regulate the numbers of species such as buffaloes, elephants, hippos and impalas. The trap was sprung when an animal stepped on a foot release at the back of the cage, causing the door to slide shut.

Bailey found that the leopards favoured riverine forests and montane habitat, with seasonal rivers being ideal as they attracted

Chui with Light and Dark. Leopards use the white underside of the tip of their tail as a signal. A mother leopard often holds her tail curled high when moving with her cubs, making it easier for them to follow her.

prey and provided good cover. The best location for traps was along riverbanks, near tributary streams or bordering firebreak roads. Leopards had more difficulty capturing prey in the dry season when there was less vegetation, increasing the chances that they would try to obtain meat from traps. During the latter half of the wet season (January and February), when newborn prey was abundant, they showed less interest in the traps.

Mothers with dependent cubs were very wary and Bailey never captured one. Other females trapped for the first time were more intent than males on escaping or attacking when approached, and were generally more aggressive and vocal.

Once a leopard had been trapped it was darted and anaesthetized, then fitted with a collar large enough to house a radio, batteries and aerial, but still weighing only 565–680gm (1¼–1½lb). Each animal was weighed, measured and fitted with neck- and ear-tags; they were then released again and their daily movements and prey recorded. Some people bridled at seeing

animals with collars and ear-tags, objecting to what they considered unnecessary interference in the lives of wild creatures in a protected area. But in those days there was little alternative if scientists were to find out more about how leopards survived in the wild.

The range of radio transmitters has improved over the years; depending on terrain the signal may be audible on headphones from several kilometres (perhaps 3–4 miles) away and up to 65km (40 miles) from the air; along with the development of satellite collars, this has opened up a whole new world to scientists. But in the '70s, radio reception was no more than 1.5–2.5km (1–1½ miles) from a vehicle and 15km (9 miles) from the air, and most radio fixes were taken within 1–2km (⅔– 1⅓ miles). Collars functioned for anything from six months to a year, whereas today batteries last for up to three years. Over the course of his two-year study Bailey drove 54,475km (34,046 miles) in his search for leopards, an average of 2,270km (1,419 miles) a month.

The first questions Bailey considered were how leopards spaced themselves and what size of area they needed. He also wanted to determine the frequency with which they killed large prey, their overall impact on prey populations and the number of impalas needed to support a given population (impalas were already known to be the leopard's principal prey in the Kruger). He captured a total of 30 leopards and was able to pinpoint their location by telemetry on 2,500 occasions, though he actually saw them only 100 times. Matters were complicated by the fact that during the day leopards often do very little other than rest in that typically nonchalant, cat-like way of theirs, lying up in a tree or under a bush, or curled up in the darkened recess of a cave, stretched out, eyes tightly shut, chin resting across their forepaw, apparently oblivious to what is going on around them. As I was to find out, the best chance of recording leopard behaviour is to find a habituated female with young cubs, when daytime activity is far more common.

While Bailey was busy radio-collaring leopards in Kruger, Patrick Hamilton, a young graduate student from the University of Nairobi, was setting about answering the same kinds of questions in Tsavo West National Park in Kenya. Hamilton employed a former poacher turned tracker for the anti-poaching unit to help him locate leopards. Elui Nthengi could find a leopard where nobody else would try; he could read the spoor that another man might not even be able to discern among the rocky outcrops and dry riverbeds in Tsavo. He could age and sex a leopard from a single pawprint, and tell you how long ago it passed this way and where it was going. Elui knew the habits of the wild creatures so well that he could even hazard a guess as to what it was going to do next, headed perhaps for a favourite waterhole or resting place, or on the track of prey.

Hamilton and Elui walked the 250 km² (100 sq. mile) study area and decided on

Half-Tail. Leopards regularly scent-mark fallen trees, rocky outcrops and bushes. First they 'read' any messages left by other leopards, then overmark the place with their own scent.

the best places to position bait to attract the leopards. Once a leopard had begun to feed, they moved the bait into a large metal box-trap. When they caught a leopard it was moved to a special wooden box designed to make it easier to inject it with an immobilizing drug. Hamilton would gingerly grasp the leopard's tail, drawing it far enough out of the box to inject it rather than trying to pierce the rump or shoulder. Within 15 minutes the leopard was drowsy enough to be removed from the box and collared. Photographs of its spot pattern were taken and various measurements recorded. The leopard would then be watched over until it had fully recovered, to prevent other predators from attacking and injuring it.

At one time Hamilton had seven different leopards radio-collared, each transmitting on a different frequency. But though he was able to track them with an aerial mounted on his Land-Rover he rarely saw them; the Tsavo leopards appeared much shyer than those in Kruger, probably because they are exposed to far fewer visitors. Of the 12 leopards that Hamilton trapped, only one was a female, though he saw a number of other females in the study area. Like Bailey, Hamilton found females to be far warier than males, and he never saw cubs. In fact the leopards were so timid that Hamilton recorded very little behaviour during his two-and-a-half-year study. He could, however, plot their movements on a map and determine how far they wandered and the extent of their home range or territory.

Both scientists noted a similar pattern in the way that male and female leopards divided up an area and used it. There appeared to be a degree of fluidity to the system. A home range might vary seasonally according to prey availability and what other leopards in the area were doing. It was maintained by subtle forms of communication such as scent-marking, scraping the ground, claw-marking trees and calling.

Both male and female leopards mark their home range by spraying, arching their tail high and squirting a stream of urine against a prominent scent-post.

Because most cats are solitary and actively avoid each other as adults, much of the information they convey to one another is by long-distance communication. Scent-marking is probably the most important of these, leaving messages that last far longer than the sound of a call. It is highly economic in that it may last for days, weeks or even months, and leaves a clear message without having to be delivered face to face, with the risk of conflict that that would entail. Though we cannot be sure exactly what a scent message tells the recipient, it seems likely that it helps to identify individuals, signal how recently they were there, whether they were young or old, male or female, and whether or not a female was in oestrus. Interestingly, young males did not seem to be unduly deterred by the scent of a big male, probably because they were either his sons and/or were not yet sexually active and unlikely to be seen as a threat.

All leopards seem to be attracted to the same kinds of prominences that serve as scent-posts: bushes, tree-stumps, overhanging branches and rocky boulders that they sniff for signs of scent before marking them. Laying down scent not only helps to communicate information to other leopards, it also has an important part to play in making an individual feel at home. As I write this at home in my study, I have just watched our cat Geronimo examining a new object– a slender box over 2m (7ft) long containing a slide-projection screen. He walked alongside it, sniffing it, rubbing his face along it and taking particular interest in its pointed ends – perfect spots to smell for signs of scent and to mark with

Zawadi relaxes in a giant fig tree overlooking Leopard Gorge – perfect leopard country. This is one of her favourite daytime resting places, with an uninterrupted view of the surrounding area.

glands situated at the corner of his mouth. If he wasn't neutered he would have sprayed it too. It was as if he were saying, 'No other cat has been here – good – I'll leave my scent and make this new feature part of my home.' All cats familiarize themselves in this way with objects in their area – be they boxes or fallen trees – incorporating them into their spatial map. The familiarity brings a sense of well-being that is probably a prerequisite for successful breeding.

Calling is another important way in which leopards advertise themselves. In Kruger adult males often called at night after scent-marking and scraping, scuffing their hind feet to leave a visible mark in the earth, using every available means to make their presence known. Leopards call when they are stationary and at times when they are walking. On flat, densely vegetated terrain in the wet season a leopard's call may be audible over no more than 1km (⅔ mile), but in the dry season on a sparsely vegetated ridge above the Sand River it could be heard from three times that distance. According to Bailey's study, the pattern of calls varied, with females giving more strokes per call, more calls per period with longer intervals between calls, and longer total call periods. Most calling occurred around dawn and dusk. The leopards seemed to be signalling their presence at the onset of their evening activity, just before they began moving around, and again when they were about to stop to rest for the day, though they have been heard calling at all hours. Not surprisingly leopards did not call near den sites or kills – locations they wanted to remain secret – but called more often when travelling well-used routes such as firebreak roads, where they might expect to encounter an adjacent territory-holder or another leopard passing through the area. Hyenas are attracted to the call of a leopard and may investigate or even follow one to try to parasitize its kills – another good reason not to call at a kill site or den.

On hearing a call a leopard may respond by joining the caller, by ignoring or avoiding it, or by answering. Females call more often when they are in oestrus, and when looking for a mate may immediately move in the direction of a male's call. In Kruger leopards called most frequently between April and June (the dry season), and least between August and January (the rainy season). This seemed to be due to seasonal changes in their environment. Calls should carry further during dry seasons when vegetation is at a minimum, and scent-marks should remain most pungent during the wet season, when high humidity reduces evaporation of scent. Hence leopards called more frequently when few scent-marks were observed and scent-marked more frequently when calling was minimal. Because leopards are such elusive and stealthy creatures, calling helps to prevent unexpected encounters, acting as an early-warning system that allows them to keep a distance, and it is probably significant that adult leopards spend most of their time 1–3km (⅔–2 miles) apart – the distance that a call can carry.

Male leopards sometimes 'duet', with both parties calling and answering, usually ending with one of them moving away to avoid confrontation. Bailey never heard subadult males calling, though they are capable of doing so by the time they are a year and a half old. Young males learn the whereabouts of territorial males by listening to their calls and taking the appropriate avoidance action. At this age they aren't yet ready to become players in the territory game, so tend to keep a low profile; adult residents find it difficult to know where subadults are if they do not call or scent-mark. Young females do not begin calling until they are 24 to 30 months old and ready to mate.

Hamilton found that adult male leopards had large territories, averaging 36 km² (14 sq. miles) and ranging from 18 to 63 km² (7–25 sq. miles), while in Kruger, Bailey found the average male territory in

Chui sheltering among the croton thickets along Dik-Dik Lugga. These seasonal watercourses provide ideal cover for a hunting leopard or a mother with small cubs.

two habitat zones to be 28 and 76 km² (11 and 30 sq. miles) respectively. The single female that Hamilton managed to radio-collar occupied a home range of 16 km² (6.25 sq. miles), very similar to Bailey's findings: the range of the single radio-collared female in one of his study areas was 18 km² (7 sq. miles), while four females in the other area averaged 15 km² (6 sq. miles). Figures for both males and females in the Mara–Serengeti are similar to this, though in some parts of Africa where prey is scarce home ranges can occupy more than 450 km² (176 sq. miles).

According to Bailey's study, not only were the ranges of adult male leopards much larger than those of females, they usually overlapped the home range of anything from one to six females. Males seemed to be trying to hold as much land as they could adequately defend against other males to enable them to breed with as many females as possible. To do this a male must try to deter others from settling in the area, and will fight if necessary. However there is often a degree of overlap around the edges of male territories, which may allow them to reach high densities

where there is enough prey to sustain them all.

Female leopards spend most of their adult life either pregnant or in the company of dependent cubs – though they often leave the cubs to their own devices. Their primary needs are a reliable supply of food, and a number of safe hiding places in which to leave small cubs when they are away hunting. But this doesn't always mean excluding other adult females from the area. In fact the home ranges of many adult females appear to overlap to a greater or lesser degree, though not because they are more social than males – they still generally make a point of avoiding other adults, regardless of sex. Avoiding that part of a home range currently occupied by another adult helps reduce competition over food. If leopards were to share hunting grounds, they would find either that prey would be hiding or that it would be ultra-alert, and too many leopards hunting in the same area would lessen the chance of any one of them obtaining a meal.

Impalas are the leopard's commonest prey in Tsavo, Kruger and much of the Mara–Serengeti. But the Tsavo leopards

also relied on small kills such as dikdiks, hares, hyraxes and various game birds, including guinea fowls and francolins. They tended to feed on the ground rather than hauling kills up into trees, no doubt because there was less likelihood of interference from lions and hyenas, which are less numerous here than they are in Mara–Serengeti. Like leopards everywhere, those in Tsavo readily killed and ate other predators, with jackals, servals, bat-eared foxes, caracals, wild cats, civets and genets all featuring on their menu.

A few years after I came to live in the Mara, an American television producer showed me some footage of Ted Bailey's study. There were some extraordinary images of the capture and radio-collaring of leopards, and one scene stays firmly in my mind – that of a leopard jumping to the ground, then springing back into the air like an acrobat and attacking the cage, as if to say, 'Take that!' Bailey describes the incident in his book *The African Leopard*:

Once an infuriated female leopard appeared to attack on release. When the trap door was opened, she attacked the upraised door, biting and clawing, but fell 1m (3ft) to the ground. She then leaped 2m (6ft 6in) up to the trap, scratched and bit the door again, and rushed a nearby vehicle. When she was 3m (10ft) away, however, she fled into nearby cover.

It was a potent reminder of just how dangerous a cornered leopard can be – far more aggressive and unpredictable than a lion, always ready to defend itself and prepared to attack at the slightest provocation.

Once one begins to understand what is important to a leopard – the basic requirements for life – it is easier to know where to start looking for them. By now I realized that a leopard's favourite areas had to provide good cover, such as rocky outcrops and hilly country where they could melt away at the first sight of danger. In the Mara, leopards often hunt along the intermittent watercourses or luggas that attract prey to pools of water, with the green and orange leaves of the croton thickets providing the perfect hiding place, though as everywhere the size of their home range varies according to the nature of the terrain and how much prey it can support. A defining moment in my quest to find a leopard was when I learned about a place called Leopard Gorge.

I'm not sure who gave the gorge its name. Perhaps it was Joseph Rotich, the Kipsigis guide at Mara River Camp, who became my mentor in all things concerning leopards – and ensured that I found my way safely back to camp each evening. Joseph was the keeper of secrets. He knew exactly what kind of country leopards preferred and where to look for them at a time when even the briefest glimpse of a leopard was more than a reward for all the hours – weeks even – of searching. Joseph was Bwana Chui – Mr Leopard – and it is hard to describe the kudos that this gave him among the other drivers. It was a good day when Joseph was in your area. He would always have something new to share.

The acacia woodland surrounding Fig Tree Ridge and Leopard Gorge is perfect leopard country. It is divided up into blocks by a series of luggas, offering a maze of cover and escape routes, with plenty of trees for a leopard confronted by lions to clamber into. There are similar woodland areas elsewhere in the Mara, but nowhere so full of character as the rocky cliffs of Fig Tree Ridge and the fortress-style architecture of Leopard Gorge. The gorge itself is concealed from view – a narrow cleft in a hillside beyond the ridge. It is so well hidden that you realize it is there only when you are almost on top of it. From it you have an unimpeded 360-degree view across the Mara. To the south you can see all the way to Musiara Marsh, and with a good pair of binoculars can pick out the tawny shapes of lions resting on a termite mound. To the north your gaze wanders past Leopard Lugga and over rising ground towards Big Wood and Military Thicket, onwards to the place where Half-Tail spent the last years of her life. To the east lie the northern extension of the Bila Shaka Lugga and Observation Hill, and further east still are Mara Buffalo Rocks, a massive rocky fortress that is another favourite leopard haunt. Across the river to the west you see the blue knife-edge of the Siria Escarpment, where Angie and I were married, a rugged strip of country that runs all the way to the Serengeti, topped by ancient fig trees and bisected by densely wooded valleys where the meat-poachers sometimes camp.

Having spent most of the day in the shade of this giant fig tree overlooking Leopard Gorge, Zawadi gets up and stretches at dusk, preparing to set off on her evening hunt.

Kisongo Masai dancing during the closing day of the *Eunoto* ceremony, when warriors have their heads shaved and become junior elders. They may now marry and own cattle.

To me Joseph was a sage, a fund of the kind of knowledge not found in the books that I was reading, the dry stuff of scientific papers detailing the extent of a leopard's home range or describing what percentage of their diet was made up of impalas. No, Joseph was dealing with the real, flesh-and-blood creature. He had for many years been a driver for filmmakers Alan and Joan Root and knew every inch of the Mara. Like George Adamson – Bwana Simba or Mr Lion – Joseph had learned to think like his quarry. He not only knew the best places to look for a leopard at first light, but also understood the way they responded when approached by a vehicle, was familiar with their favourite hiding places. He realized, and made me realize, that if you wanted to watch leopards you needed to be patient – as patient as the leopard itself.

Leopard Gorge and the rocky outcrop to its west known as Fig Tree Ridge lie beyond the Mara Reserve boundary. This land belongs to the Masai – as does the reserve itself, which is held in trust on their behalf by the Kenya Government. In the 1970s the land surrounding the Mara was owned on a communal basis, divided into large group ranches that were owned collectively by a number of families. All that has now changed. The group ranches are being subdivided and individual title given to the people. Conservationists worry that some of the land will be sold to agriculturalists and ploughed up, that fences will divide the land and that wildlife will disappear as the Masai adopt a more sedentary lifestyle. If, as seems inevitable, this happens, the Masai will lose the opportunity to capitalize on some of the finest game country in Africa; a priceless heritage will be destroyed in exchange for a pittance compared to its true value.

In the old days, the leopards living in these northern ranchlands actually benefited from the Masai's pastoral lifestyle. There are fewer lions and hyenas living outside the reserve, where they have to compete with the pastoralists for living space, and for as long as there are plenty of impalas and Thomson's gazelles in the area, leopards have little reason to take livestock.

Leopard Gorge and Fig Tree Ridge fall within an area designated for photographic safaris, not trophy-hunting. But that didn't stop the killing in the bad old days. Leopards were shot illegally by unscrupulous trophy-hunters sanctioned by corrupt officials, and by poachers eager to earn the price of another spotted coat. Little wonder that it was so hard to find a leopard when I first came to live at Mara River Camp. At least Joseph knew where to look. He told me that there was nowhere better to start than Leopard Gorge and Fig

Tree Ridge. This was very different country to Musiara Marsh and the Bila Shaka Lugga where we searched for lions. That is open country, bounded by riverine forest in the west and rolling plains to the east, dissected by the narrow intermittent watercourse known as Bila Shaka Lugga, which is shaded by dense croton thickets and the occasional tree or clump of woodland. Here the Marsh Lions could invariably be found, exuding the confidence that their size and numbers allowed them. Occasionally – if you were very lucky – someone might report seeing a leopard skulking among the forested river's edge or in the densest part of the lugga.

But as you travelled north beyond the Musiara entrance gate, the country changed. Where before you could see a predator moving about from a couple of kilometres or more, now the country crowded in around you, a mosaic of tightly packed acacia bushes and elegant eleaodendron trees, leaving just enough space for you to squeeze through in a Toyota Landcruiser, the long thorns snagging and scraping against your paintwork. Here there were more trees of every description, giant figs and euphorbias hugging the rim of Fig Tree Ridge, as well as sweet-smelling, crimson-flowered kigelia – the sausage trees with their huge cream-coloured pods. At night I would lie in my tent dreaming of the day when I might find a leopard resting in one of these trees and photograph it. Occasionally I would awake to the sound of a leopard's distinctive rasping call. But I was to wait six years before being able to achieve my ambition.

On our walks up the Siria Escarpment, Angie and I would often see fresh signs of leopards – claw marks gouged deep into the bark of a tree, or tufts of fur plucked from a kill before the leopard began to eat. I would sometimes climb into one of the fig trees and lie along a massive limb, looking out over the Mara 300m (1,000ft) below me, imaging myself to be the leopard that just hours earlier had lain here, smelling

the musky scent it had sprayed against the tree trunk as it passed on its way.

A number of leopards shared this area. That I knew from listening to Joseph. Finding a leopard was a gift Joseph could bestow on a safari that few other people could match in those days. In fact the other drivers made a point of tracking Joseph down when he was in residence to find out what he had seen. Joseph guarded his secrets carefully. If he knew that a particular driver wasn't respectful in his approach to wildlife he kept his information to himself. But if the driver was careful in the way he went about his business, then Joseph would tell him what he had seen, cautioning him to *chunga* – to be careful not to disturb the leopard. He hated to see a mob of vehicles crowding any of the big cats and never allowed his clients to talk loudly in their presence. Joseph could silence people simply by raising his finger to his lips, or touching the leg of someone standing out of the roof hatch. They would know from his expression to sit down and keep quiet, that being in the presence of a leopard was something special and worthy of respect.

It took me a while to find my way unerringly to Leopard Gorge, but in time I came to recognize the clump of trees guarding its western entrance. It made little

difference to my success in seeing a leopard, though. Meanwhile, Joseph regaled me with tales of the resident female – a big leopard with a coat the colour of burnished oak. The male whose territory overlapped hers was himself a huge animal, with the massive head so typical of an adult male leopard, a pronounced, dog-like muzzle and a heavy dewlap of skin around his throat. He was instantly recognizable due to his opaque wall-eye. This gave him a particularly fierce look, adding to his presence and magnifying the intensity of the stare from his one good eye. I saw him only on a handful of occasions. But that was all one could hope for in those days, a brief glimpse simply increasing the excitement that leopards inspired in me.

The turning point in my love affair with leopards came one morning in July 1978 when Joseph told me that a female had been sighted with two small cubs in the Leopard Gorge area. It seemed certain that this must be the shy creature on whom I had yet to set eyes. Her cubs were occasionally spotted peering from the entrance to one of the many caves in the gorge. Joseph thought they must be about four months old. Eventually, after many days of searching, my luck changed and I had my first glimpse of the cubs as they

The Mara Buffalo female – Chui's mother. This is one of the few photographs I managed to take of this shy leopard.

Chui's younger sister watching a hyena emerge from a cave at Mara Buffalo Rocks. Leopards and hyenas use this area as a resting place and to hide their young.

crouched over the carcass of a wildebeest calf their mother had killed. The calf was too heavy for her to hoist into the leafy crown of the nearby eleaodendron tree, so she had left it on the ground. After opening the carcass and feeding from it for a while, she must have called her cubs and led them to the kill.

As I drove along the top of the gorge she watched me from her hiding place high up

in the tree – ideally positioned to detect the approach of danger. I had no clue as to her whereabouts until I saw a blur of spots descending the trunk of the tree and disappearing into the gorge 30m (100ft) away. The cubs ignored their mother's sudden departure – they were far less nervous of vehicles than she was. I sat watching them, their faces bloody from feasting. I never took my eyes off them as I

reached for my camera, but the movement was too much for them and they bolted for the gorge.

I would not see the mother again for five years, though I knew she was still in the area. Joseph would occasionally find her, and every so often I would see one or other of the cubs, a male and a female. The female cub I named Chui, which is Swahili for leopard. She was the first of a new generation of leopards that had no reason to fear people in vehicles, and would in the years to come allow me an intimate glimpse of her life.

Chui mated for the first time when she was two and a half years old, and in January 1981 gave birth to two cubs in a cave hidden away in the middle of a huge rocky fortress at the eastern entrance to Leopard Gorge – the same place that Zawadi would use as the hiding place for her third litter some 20 years later. I never managed to discover the sex of Chui's cubs, though one was lighter in colour than the other. They were about ten weeks old when Joseph first found them, and for a while the two of us skulked around the vicinity of the gorge whenever we could, trying not to precipitate a flood of vehicles that would almost certainly have forced the mother to move the cubs.

In the end our caution was of little consequence. Members of the Gorge Pride discovered Chui's hiding place, sniffing at the entrance to the cave and prowling around the rocks in the most menacing manner. Fortunately Chui must have sensed the danger and moved her cubs before any harm could come to them.

I saw them one last time towards the end of the long rains in the middle of May, when they were six months old. From the upper reaches of a diospyros tree along Leopard Lugga, not far from the gorge, they stared down at me with a mixture of curiosity and wariness. Shortly afterwards a lioness surprised Chui and her cubs along this same lugga, forcing them to seek the safety of the treetops. Though Chui and one of the cubs managed to escape into the trees, the other reacted a fraction too late and was trapped in a thicket and killed.

This was the first of many incidents that made me realize how dangerous lions are to leopards of all ages. I never discovered if the remaining cub survived to adulthood, though I think it probably did, as the next time Chui gave birth was two and a half years later.

I was lying flat on my back in England recovering from a back operation when the moment I had been waiting for arrived unexpectedly one September morning in 1983. A friend wrote to say that two leopards had given birth to cubs within 6.5km (4 miles) of each other. If anything was destined to speed up my recovery this was it. The two leopards turned out to be Chui and her mother – the shy female I later named the Mara Buffalo female. She had given birth to a male and a female cub early in the year, choosing as her den site the Mara Buffalo Rocks – hence her name. Six months later Chui produced two male cubs in a cave along Fig Tree Ridge.

At last I was able to watch a leopard on a regular basis. I would drive to Fig Tree Ridge at dawn each morning and stay there until darkness drove me back to camp. There were times, after all the tourists had left, when Chui would emerge from one of her favourite fig trees or walk out of the lugga, calling her cubs to join her and making the many hours I had spent cramped in my vehicle more than worthwhile.

I named Chui's cubs Light and Dark, acknowledging the colour of their coats, though I soon discovered that they had personalities as different as their markings. Light was somewhat nervous and timid, while Dark was bold and adventurous and generally dominated his brother when play became rough or there was a dispute over food. All that changed when the cubs were

Light and Dark playing at the Cub Caves – a perfect location to hide young cubs.

Dark at six months old. He was bolder and more inquisitive than his brother Light.

about four months old and Dark hurt himself in a fall, badly wrenching and spraining one of his back legs. This was a devastating injury and at times Chui was forced to carry the crippled cub in her mouth. For all their marvellous climbing ability, even adult leopards occasionally tumble from trees. Although they normally land safely on their padded paws, they do sometimes sustain injuries – more often to their face and jaw than to their shock-absorbent limbs. After his accident, Dark was no longer able to dominate Light. Suddenly the tables were turned and it was Light's turn to gain the upper hand, providing a graphic example of how life's uncertainties can mould and change the individual. I wrote about the incident in *The Leopard's Tale*:

It was pathetic to watch as Dark tried to follow his mother. Every step seemed to cause him pain and Light just would not leave him alone. He pounced on his helpless brother and wrestled him to the ground, holding him down by biting him in the neck and throat. Weakened by his injury, Dark's only defence was to lie as still as possible, waiting for his brother to tire of the game. But the moment he tried to crawl forward to reach Chui's teats, the movement stimulated Light even further – just like a cat playing with an injured mouse.

It was noticeable that Light had at last started to lose some of his shyness. He was full of playfulness, chasing up and down in the croton bushes and pestering Dark. Light seemed instilled with a new source of energy, leaping and exploding into the air like a jack-in-a-box. It was difficult to know if this new-found confidence and vigour was a consequence of Dark's injury or just the natural process of Light's own development. Whichever it was, Light exploited to the full the opportunity to dominate Dark whilst his brother was less than a hundred per cent fit. "

Two weeks later I watched as Chui returned from one of her hunting excursions with the hindquarters of a freshly killed impala fawn clasped firmly in her jaws. She called the cubs from their hiding place along Fig Tree Ridge, and both immediately emerged and ran towards her, with Dark still noticeably limping. The minute Chui dropped the kill, Dark grabbed it and carried it into the bushes; he was thinner than his brother and hadn't eaten for a number of days. Meanwhile, Light was forced to content himself with a suckle and a lick from his mother. When he tried to approach his brother, Dark turned on him, chasing after him on his three good legs and bowling him over. Chui tried to intervene, but the cubs rolled away from her. Over and over they tumbled, biting and clawing, neither giving way, until they finally broke apart. Dark rushed back to the kill, protectively straddling it and threatening both his relatives not to come any closer.

But it wasn't over yet. After Dark had fed for a while, his tummy bulging with meat, he walked over to Light and in a friendly gesture rubbed against his brother's head. But Light was only interested in the remains of the kill, trying to slide surreptitiously past his brother. Seeing this, Dark quickly moved back to the meat, then just as quickly moved away again. Light took his chance and this time when Dark tried to return he had lost the initiative. Now the food was Light's possession and he quickly leapt forward to defend it. The brothers fought fiercely for nearly a minute in a manner that I had never observed amongst lion cubs, whose quarrels were usually resolved as soon as they started, or cheetahs, who never behaved in this manner at a kill. The leopard is a creature apart.

*D*istinguishing individual cubs – both physically and in terms of their temperaments – is much easier with leopards than with lions or cheetahs. Lionesses in the same pride often breed at the same time, particularly when new pride males have killed any young cubs, prompting the females to come into oestrus again. This means that there may be a dozen or more cubs of a similar age being raised communally in a crèche. The fact that lionesses often allow their relatives' cubs to suckle from them, and that small cubs all look so similar, makes it very difficult to identify and keep track of individuals among the crèche until they are six months or older. Cheetahs may have up to eight cubs in a litter, so although each has a different pattern of rings and spots on its tail as well as different spot markings on its face and body, it can take time to sort out which individual is which. In contrast, leopards normally have only two cubs, occasionally three, and each cub quickly establishes a teat order, making it relatively easy to tell them apart, particularly if one is male and one is female. The spot markings are useful too – Zawadi, for instance, is easy to recognize because of the row of five identical spots beneath her right eye. The fact that leopard cubs are often very different in character also helps distinguish one from another. They may be shy or bold, cautious or adventurous, some quickly becoming relaxed with vehicles while others, such as Zawadi's daughter Safi, remain wary and nervous throughout their lives.

Dark and Light at five months, waiting for their mother to return from hunting.

Chui in her prime at six years old. She was the first
leopard that I was able to observe closely.

The Paradise Female

Following Chui and her cubs was the highlight of those early years living in the Mara. It was the fulfilment of all that I had hoped for. I dreaded the moment when it might end – and sure enough, when Light and Dark were six months old, Chui moved away from Fig Tree Ridge. Despite all our efforts we failed to find her new hiding place. But finally, after six years of waiting, I had sufficient photographs to illustrate their story.

Having completed *The Leopard's Tale* I spent much of the next few years in Tanzania, documenting the story of the wildebeest migration as it moved back and forth between the Serengeti's southern plains and the Masai Mara. This enabled me to fulfil another of my ambitions – watching packs of wild dogs when they paused long enough from their nomadic wanderings to establish a den and breed.

Even though months might pass when I was unable to visit the Mara and my old haunts around Musiara Marsh and Leopard Gorge, I kept in close contact with what was happening in the lives of key animal characters in these areas. I still held out hope that Chui would reappear and that I would have the chance to follow her when she had her next litter of cubs.

But she didn't. It wasn't until almost two years later that I had word of her again. In October 1985 friends told me that a leopard with three cubs had been seen in Leopard Gorge. She was rather shy, though the cubs were old enough occasionally to venture forth from their hiding place in one of the caves. They were about three months old, the same age as Light and Dark had been when I first saw them. I immediately went in search of the leopards, and sure enough one morning found the cubs playing on a slab of rock halfway along the gorge – close to where Chui and her brother had been born in 1978. As the sun soared higher into the sky the cubs retreated again to their rocky hideaway. I stayed, hoping that sooner or later their mother would return.

Light greeting his mother in typical cat fashion, pushing his head and body under her throat and winding his tail around her neck, wafting his scent in her face.

Later that afternoon I heard the piercing alarm call of a bush hyrax, and turned to see a leopard walking cautiously along the top of the gorge. She paused to drink from a rocky depression where rainwater had collected, and I studied her through my binoculars, wondering who she might be. Perhaps it was Chui's younger sister, one of the two cubs born to the Mara Buffalo female in late 1982, who would by now be nearly three years old. But this leopard was older than that, thicker set and with one or two black spots on her pink nose. I'm not sure why I didn't immediately recognize her as Chui – perhaps because she appeared so wary, even though I was nowhere near her, on the far side of the gorge.

At one point she turned towards me, bared her teeth and hissed, telling me to keep my distance. I moved back and watched as she continued on her way. She was behaving just as I would have expected a leopard with young cubs to behave, stopping every so often to look around, checking to make sure that she hadn't been seen by lions or hyenas, anxious not to reveal the hiding place of her young. As she drew nearer I could just make out the soft puffing sound she often used to let her family know that she was home. Instantly three cubs appeared on the top of the rocks above the cave where they had been waiting patiently. They greeted their mother in a frenzy of excitement, pushing up under her chin and winding themselves sinuously around her chest and legs as she licked them. Then she lay down, making a point of not letting them suckle. Perhaps she had made a kill and would lead them to it later, but for the moment she seemed content to rest, while the cubs busied themselves scrambling about in the bushes that sprouted from the top of the rocks, biting and playing with one another.

I still didn't realize that this was Chui. Only many months later while looking through some photographs taken that morning did I pick up a copy of *The Leopard's Tale* and compare the spot markings of this leopard with Chui's – they

The Mara Buffalo Female's year-old cubs in 1984. By this age male cubs (left) are noticeably bigger and heavier than their sisters.

were identical. I was overjoyed at the thought of this chance meeting with my old friend, who by now was seven years old and in her prime – this was her third litter of cubs. I had sometimes wondered if she had been killed, and had often dreamed of seeing her again and perhaps finding out what had happened to Light and Dark. Watching Chui with her new litter convinced me that Light and Dark must have survived – at least to the point where they were old enough to become independent from their mother. The timing was perfect. They had been born in June 1983, two years before the arrival of these three cubs. Eighteen months to two years is the typical interval between litters for a leopard if the youngsters survive.

Any ideas that I might have had of repeating my success in following Chui and her new litter soon evaporated. She and her cubs were seen once more a few days later at the Cub Caves along Fig Tree Ridge, the same site where she had spent so much time with Light and Dark. Looking back on that period I now realize that Chui probably simply moved further to the north or east, seeking sanctuary in the area that Half-Tail and Zawadi ended up using – the rocky hideaways beyond Mara River airstrip. Very few tourist vehicles bothered to search

here. There was so much to be seen in the Musiara area and its surrounds that there was little need for drivers to invest time patrolling country that others rarely frequented: part of the key to a successful game drive is to tap into the network of information provided by other vehicles.

I did, however, occasionally manage to catch up with Chui's younger brother and sister. The female could sometimes be found between Mara Buffalo Rocks and Fig Tree Ridge, an area she shared with her mother and sister, as well as wandering further to the north where some years later she succeeded in raising a single cub. Her brother developed into a magnificent young male. On one occasion I watched him feeding on a full-grown female topi, which weighed in the region of 110kg (240lb) – double his weight – that he had dragged into a thick patch of croton. The carcass was too big to haul into a tree, and anyway there wasn't a suitable tree close at hand, so he feasted on the ground until he looked fit to burst. At one point he was surprised by a group of young lions who must have smelt the kill, or heard him methodically gnawing through the rib-ends, and sneaked up on him. The lions were two-year-olds, large enough to kill a leopard – but he was saved by a driver from Mara

Buffalo Camp, who launched his vehicle straight at the lions, scattering them and giving the male time to escape.

That was very much the way things were for the next four years – an occasional glimpse of a leopard with days or even weeks between sightings. Nevertheless, a number of leopards scattered through the Mara had become accustomed to vehicles, though there was no guarantee that you would find them. The Talek River, a tributary of the Mara, was a favourite place to search, offering plenty of cover for a hunting leopard; so too were the dense thickets and rocky hills on the southern reaches of Paradise Plain near the wildebeest river-crossing sites. Leopards were also sometimes seen along the Siria Escarpment or in the riverine thickets bordering the Mara River. But trying to keep track of a leopard is a painstaking business, and few people have the time or inclination to go out doggedly each day and cover every inch of a home range. Nowhere was there a leopard that could offer the kind of opportunities we had enjoyed with Chui.

Then one day word began to spread that a new leopard was being seen around Fig Tree Ridge and Leopard Gorge, a leopard you could watch if you could find her – a leopard like Chui. I could hardly wait to see who this 'new' leopard might be. By all accounts she was one of two cubs who had been born in a rocky outcrop to the south of Governor's Camp and whose mother occupied a home range bordering the southern reaches of Paradise Plain. If this was true then she had moved 20km (12 miles) from her normal haunts, which at the time I found surprising. Young females often remain in the area where they are born, just as Chui had done, overlapping part of their mother's home range or establishing themselves close by. But a move of 20km (12 miles) is not beyond the realms of possibility – male leopards sometimes make a journey of that distance in a single night as they move around their territory, and young leopards of both sexes must sometimes seek new areas if they are to breed successfully. However, Fig Tree Ridge and Leopard Gorge – Chui's old haunts – were such prime leopard habitat that I would not have thought that a stranger to the area would find much room available. I looked forward to finding out more about this new leopard, whom the drivers at Governor's Camp had named the Paradise female.

There was one other leopard whom we occasionally saw skulking around the area, a shy female who in April 1990 had given birth to two cubs – a male and female – in the Cub Caves along Fig Tree Ridge. I don't know what happened to the female cub, but, unlike his mother, the male became quite tolerant of being viewed. I felt certain that this older leopard couldn't be the Paradise female's mother. Any leopard as relaxed around vehicles as she was must have grown up in the presence of a mother with a similar attitude. But then I thought about how shy the Mara Buffalo female had been compared to her daughter Chui.

Regardless of where she came from or who her mother was, everyone agreed that the Paradise female was something special. Even Chui had never been as amenable as this. The Paradise female was about two and a half years old when I first saw her in early 1990, a normal age for a leopard to produce her first litter. She had recently mated with the territorial male, and we all anxiously awaited the arrival of her cubs.

Sadly, it is not unusual for any cat to lose its first litter, and the Paradise female proved to be no exception. She was seen one morning emerging from a thicket to the east of Leopard Gorge, looking very distressed. She was plainly no longer pregnant, but no sign was ever seen of any cubs. As I wrote at the time:

Perhaps her cubs had been stillborn, or she had chosen her den unwisely: it is not uncommon for cats and dogs to fail to raise their first litter due to

Half-Tail (before she lost her tail) rests in a balanites tree early one morning. A Thomson's gazelle kill is stashed safely out of sight in the tree beside her.

inexperience. Lions or hyenas – even baboons – would certainly penalize the slightest error in judgement on the part of a mother leopard who failed to conceal her newborn cubs carefully.

Surprisingly, perhaps, baboons can be a real menace to leopards, particularly females with young cubs. It has often been said that baboons are the favourite prey of leopards, and certainly leopards do kill baboons at times. But in all my years of watching leopards I have rarely seen one with a baboon kill and have come to have a healthy respect for the monkeys' ability to look after themselves in their dealings with leopards – at least during daylight hours.

The Paradise Female 49

Adult male baboons weigh 27kg (60lb) or more – some as much as 45kg (100lb), equal to a leopard the size of the Paradise female. Most monkeys spend their lives in trees, only occasionally foraging on the ground, but baboons are unusual in that they spend much of their time searching for food on the open savannas or among the acacia thickets, eating a wide variety of vegetable matter, particularly short green grass and ripe fruits such as figs, as well as grubs and termite alates, birds' eggs and nestlings; adult male baboons also sometimes kill and eat young gazelles, impalas and hares. At the first sign of danger, baboons emit a loud bark, immediately attracting the attention of troop members, who respond either by taking avoidance action or by rallying to counter the threat. The big males quickly challenge a predator such as a leopard, ganging up on it and chasing it away. This mobbing behaviour is highly effective in ensuring that the leopard hunts elsewhere, allowing the baboons to continue feeding in relative safety.

A large male baboon is a bold, brave and dangerous adversary, confident in its ability to scare off a leopard – particularly the smaller females. I watched numerous hostile encounters between Chui and baboons from the Fig Tree Troop, who included Fig Tree Ridge and Leopard Gorge in their home range. The giant fig trees provided the perfect roost for the troop when they were in the area, and every few days they would return to the ridge and take up residence at their chosen sleeping place. They knew all about Chui, and made a point of harassing her throughout the six months that she stayed at the Cub Caves with Light and Dark. Eventually an uneasy truce developed, ensuring that neither baboons nor leopards sustained injury, though there were a few close calls. Many was the time that Chui was caught in the open and had to run for one of the caves – though it often seemed as if the baboons did not actually want to lay hands on her. Safely inside the cave, Chui would hiss and snarl at the mob, forced to endure the taunts of the younger males, who were always quick to exploit the situation.

On one memorable occasion members of the troop joined Chui in the top of one of her favourite fig trees, nonchalantly plucking ripe figs from among the branches, forcing her to retreat to the topmost limbs and tuck her legs beneath her. Eventually she lost her nerve – or had simply had enough – charging down past the baboons, who fled screaming and chattering as she streaked past them and disappeared into the Cub Caves.

In 1992, something happened that was to mark the Paradise female out for the rest of her life. She lost her tail. Nobody knows for certain how this happened – baboons have to be high on the list of potential assailants, though it may have been the

Male baboons weigh 30–35 kg (66–77 lb), almost as much as most female leopards. This yawn is really a threat, exposing dagger-like canines.

*O*n one occasion the young male leopard I sometimes happened upon in the area found himself cornered by baboons in Leopard Gorge. He lay on a rock watching as the baboons moved closer, and then instead of disappearing into one of the caves took up a position crouched in a clump of long grass.

I could barely see him as he flattened himself against the ground, but the baboons were not to be denied the satisfaction of forcing him to flee. They crowded onto the rocks above him, becoming more and more agitated and vociferous as their number swelled – the sounds of their barks and screams rising in an intimidating crescendo. Surely the young male must give ground and run for safety. But he wasn't moving. Sometimes a leopard will hold its ground simply so as not to provoke a chase, ready to defend itself if it must, but hoping that the danger will fade away. Not this time. One of the big male baboons jumped down into the grass no more than a metre or so from the young leopard, thumb-sized canines bared right in his face, shrieking and grunting as loudly as he could. The leopard responded with an explosive cough, prompting the baboon to leap high into the air, giving him time to turn and disappear from view. He was lucky; baboons have been known to kill leopards, even adult males.

Chui sheltering from baboons. In the Mara leopards do everything possible to avoid confrontation with these powerful monkeys.

result of a scrap with another cat. Female leopards do sometimes fight with a rival over turf, though the lack of visible injuries to most of the females I have watched (they look far less battered than many lionesses) indicates that fighting is uncommon and rarely life-threatening. That said, the consequences of being forced to leave an area can be serious. Wounds to the rump and tail are a common feature of cat fights, with the combatants slashing and biting at one another, particularly when a solitary individual is forced to face off against more than one rival, as happens when lions corner an adversary. While one lion confronts its opponent head on, others try to get in behind it to inflict maximum injury to its exposed hindquarters. If the Paradise female's wound was the result of a fight with lions, then she was lucky to escape with her life. Lions are ruthlessly efficient in inflicting damage on their competitors and kill cheetahs and leopards whenever the chance arises.

I could easily envisage how baboons might have surprised the Paradise female,

having photographed a previous incident when she was forced to flee from a gang of them. On another occasion I had seen her race for her life along the top of Leopard Gorge, pursued by two or three large males, one of whom reached out and grabbed at her tail and rump, forcing her to flip on to her back to defend herself, before slithering to safety among the rocks.

Friends sent me photographs of the Paradise female after her injury. Her beautiful spotted tail had been left hanging limply like a broken branch, almost severed in two. Eventually two-thirds of her tail were lost and from that day onwards she became know as Half-Tail. But if she suffered any undue consequences it was never apparent. She continued to hunt and

Half-Tail being chased by male baboons. Although she reached the safety of a thicket, this may have been how she lost part of her tail.

A year-old male leopard with a Thomson's gazelle that his mother had killed. At this age young leopards are also beginning to hunt small prey for themselves.

enables them to keep a constant check on the sexual readiness of the females living in their area, and helps to ensure that they are in a position to drive away any wandering males who might find an oestrus female before they do. This is vital from the male's point of view, as a female on heat is promiscuous and liable to mate with any male of her choosing; in areas where males have overlapping territories a female may end up mating with two or three males in one oestrus. But as biologist Luke Hunter pointed out to me, mating with more than one male probably helps to confuse paternity, lessening the chance that a male might try to harm any cubs produced from the liaison.

Normally subadult males have little opportunity to mate until they acquire a territory of their own at around three to four years of age. Prior to this they wisely adopt a low profile, rarely scent-marking or calling and thereby reducing the chance of a hostile reception from the territory-holder (who may be their father) and giving themselves the opportunity to stay in their natal range for as long as possible. But sometimes they have little choice in the matter, as happened when Half-Tail lost her first litter. Unknown to her, the territorial male had recently been killed by Masai herdsmen in retaliation for an attack on a herdboy. This caused a temporary vacuum, and Half-Tail was unable to find a suitable mate in her normal range. One day we found her in Leopard Gorge, attempting to mate with the young male leopard born to

climb trees with all her old athleticism, and her cubs found her stumpy tail just as irresistible a plaything as it was when it was still intact.

Half-Tail provided us with the opportunity to observe a female leopard throughout her adult life. She produced six litters – 14 cubs in all – and raised three cubs to adulthood. When she wasn't pregnant or accompanied by cubs she would come into oestrus every 20 to 50 days until she conceived again, with oestrus lasting anything from a few days to a week and a gestation period of 90–105 days.

Cats are induced ovulators, releasing an egg only once mating commences, an adaptation to the solitary existence that most male and female cats lead. Induced ovulation allows time for a female and male to find each other before the female ovulates. A female on heat becomes restless, ranging more widely as she searches for a mate, scent-marking and calling frequently, often pausing to rub her head and face against rocky promontories and bushes, sometimes rolling on the ground. The fact that male leopards move around their territories relatively rapidly – in some cases every four or five days –

The young male was killed by lions from the Gorge Pride when he was 18 months old.

the shy female who shared part of the same area. Half-Tail must have linked up with the male and was now trying to seduce him. At one point she mounted him, biting the skin on his nape and thrusting with her hindquarters. Both leopards sniffed and sprayed, each intrigued by the other's scent. But the male wasn't yet sexually mature – the earliest instance of a male mating successfully is at two years of age – and so Half-Tail failed to become pregnant. That was the closest the young male ever got to siring cubs. A few months later he was killed by members of the Gorge Pride, when a vehicle flushed him from cover, revealing his hiding place to the lions resting nearby.

In prime leopard habitat there is rarely a vacuum for long. There is nearly always a reservoir of male leopards – young or old – ready to capitalize on a vacant territory, and in time a new male took over the territory and mated with Half-Tail. Both Bailey and Hamilton noted that although young male leopards sometimes made exploratory forays well beyond their natal area, they often returned, at least until they were almost adult. But when a vacancy occurred it was invariably a leopard from outside the area who took over. The ownership of male territories seemed generally to be quite stable, with established males maintaining their ranges for a number of years, though not as long as resident females.

Half-Tail was five years old when she gave birth to her second litter along Fig Tree Ridge on 3 November 1992. Three cubs were seen initially, though one of them is thought to have been killed by a lion, possibly the second one too. The third, a female, survived. The German photographer Fritz Polking was so entranced by her that he named her Beauty.

It was just like old times, reminding me of days spent watching Chui with Light and Dark. After a gap of nearly ten years, here at last was another leopard with a cub whom we could observe and photograph on a daily basis, at least for as long as she remained in one locality. In my experience leopard cubs are at their most photogenic

Half-Tail and Beauty early one morning near Leopard Gorge.

Leopard cubs weigh 430–1000g (1–2lb) at birth and their eyes open in their second week. They begin to scramble around in bushes and onto tree stumps from the time they are about six weeks old, and by three months they can climb up into most trees, which often proves to be a life-saving ploy. A mother leopard sometimes brings small prey or a part of a carcass back to where she has left her cubs, though at two months they pick at the meat rather than really eating it and still prefer to suckle when they can. But by the time they are three months old they really begin to tuck in, and are old enough to be led to a kill (some females start to bring their cubs to a kill from as early as eight weeks). Once the carcass is finished the female often moves the cubs to a new lair before setting off to hunt again, unless she has the luxury of a place like Fig Tree Ridge or Leopard Gorge that offers longer stays if needed. Cubs are virtually weaned at four months and their mother becomes increasingly reluctant to let them suckle, baring her teeth and hissing her disapproval, refusing to roll onto her side despite their noisy protests. The cubs still try to suckle for another month or so, though they probably gain very little milk by this stage, just the comfort of lying close to their mother and making contact with her. By now she may be absent for two or three days at a time, reaffirming her claim to her home range and searching for food. If she has been unsuccessful then she may move with the cubs to a new area before setting off to hunt again. The introduction to a solitary existence starts early.

Light and Dark at four months old feasting on a warthog piglet. Cubs do not like to share food, usually taking it in turns to feed.

between the ages of six weeks and six months. This is certainly the best time to photograph them with their mother – with lots of lovely greetings and play sessions.

It is not uncommon for a leopard to move her cubs on an almost daily basis during the first few weeks of their lives, in an attempt to prevent their scent from building up and attracting predators. Leopards have a very distinctive scent and any passing lion or hyena would be able to tell that one was in residence – as would smaller predators such as mongooses and civets, who would certainly be capable of killing young cubs. Hyenas in particular have such a well-developed sense of smell and are such inquisitive creatures that they would soon notice if a leopard remained in the same place for any length of time. Both Fig Tree Ridge and Leopard Gorge have

long found favour with lions and hyenas as well as leopards, providing birthplaces for their own young and cool resting places to lie up in the heat of the day. Today Leopard Gorge is like hyena city, as Zawadi found to her cost when trying to raise a litter here in August 2002. All it took was one risky move to a cave with a wide open mouth. Attracted by the smell of a Thomson's gazelle kill that Zawadi had stashed in a nearby tree, the hyenas must have tracked her to the place where she had left her cubs, who were less than a month old. Though she managed to carry one of the cubs to safety, the other two perished. Anything that disturbs a mother leopard's equilibrium is liable to prompt her to move her cubs – whether it be discovery by vehicles, people moving through the area on foot or predators.

Angie and I were able to watch Half-Tail and Beauty for a number of weeks in the early part of 1993. By then they had become localized around a series of three low hills near the northern end of Ngorbop Lugga, close to where the Masai had speared the old male leopard and where the young male had been killed by the Gorge Pride in 1991. The rocky, bush-covered hills and nearby lugga offered numerous escape routes for mother and cub when the inevitable confrontations with lions, hyenas and baboons occurred. There was plenty of prey here too, with herds of Thomson's gazelles and impalas always somewhere within view, as well as smaller fare such as dikdiks and hares.

We would try to reach the three hills each morning before sun-up, scouring the rocks and bushes for any signs of movement, listening for the tell-tale yelping barks of black-backed jackals that might signal that a leopard was afoot, and glassing the surrounding plains for indications that the herds of prey were in any way disturbed. Often there was nothing – nothing except for the sound of a hyena whooping or the distant roaring of lions. As the sun began to edge towards the horizon, white-bellied bustards competed with coqui francolins, uttering harsh grating calls that marked their position out on the plains or among the acacia woodlands, contrasting sharply with the liquid notes of white-browed robin chats invisible among the dense undergrowth of the lugga.

There is a chill to the morning air in Africa. A leopard who has been active during the night may still be huddled, scrunched up for warmth among the bushes or on a rocky ledge – better still, tucked away in a cave, emerging only to warm itself briefly once the sun is up before disappearing from view again. We quickly learned that just because we couldn't see Half-Tail or Beauty – however hard we looked – it didn't mean that they weren't there. If we simply revisited the same places time and again, sooner or later one of them would appear. By now Beauty was six months old, could easily climb the tallest tree and was used to being left on her own for long periods. Beauty was confident enough to show herself to vehicles – or at least to ignore them and continue her normal routine. For a leopard of this age this means becoming more and more involved with its immediate environment, stalking small prey such as lizards and birds, watching larger prey that might pass by, even creeping up on animals such as buffaloes and elephants that sometimes passed through the thickets where Beauty spent her days.

With no siblings to play with, Beauty was forced to amuse herself, wiling away the many hours – days even – when her mother was absent. She invented all manner of games with sticks, rocks and

Light perched on top of a dead tree he had clambered up in order to chase a tawny eagle. Leopard cubs are inquisitive and are used to being left to their own devices.

animal droppings, leaping into the air to launch attacks on plants and bushes, clasping them between her over-sized forepaws and collapsing onto her back, scampering up and down trees, chewing on twigs and dabbing at pebbles and elephant droppings. Sometimes she would whip herself into such a frenzy that she reminded us of a hyperactive child, performing somersaults, twists – anything was possible. Slow-moving creatures such as pangolins and porcupines were particularly attractive, though porcupines are something that leopards have to learn to treat with caution. Beauty loved nothing better than when a tortoise blundered into view, a harmless

Dark, aged five months, playing with a leopard tortoise along Fig Tree Ridge.

'rock' that could be gnawed or up-ended, forcing her to wrinkle her nose and curl her lip in an exaggerated grimace or flehmen face as the tortoise responded to the shock by releasing a stream of foul-smelling liquid from its cloaca. The best moments were when Half-Tail eventually returned from her wanderings. After the mandatory greeting session between mother and cub with Beauty sinuously rubbing her head and flank against her mother, a period of grooming would give way to play-fighting, which both leopards clearly relished. This was a chance for us to witness, close up, the extraordinary athleticism, speed of reflex and agility that leopards possess. They are just so quick.

Most leopards become semi-independent by the time they are a year to a year and a half old. By this stage their mother is likely to be pregnant again. It has

always been assumed that lions, leopards and cheetahs – perhaps all cats – do not come into oestrus as long as they have dependent cubs. Yet females do usually mate again before their cubs become independent, and where leopards are concerned the arrival of a new litter normally puts an end to further contact

with or provision of food for the older offspring. Kate Nicholls and Pieter Kat, who for the past few years have conducted lion research in the Okavango Delta in Botswana, question the assumption that big cats remain anoestrus while they have cubs, believing that, in the case of lions at least, females continue to cycle but that those

Dark and Light at six months, play-fighting. At this age cubs often wrestle and practise the killing bite that they will use on prey.

with dependent cubs simply avoid mating when they are in season, rather than not cycling at all. Support for their work comes from faecal analysis, allowing traces of reproductive hormones to be monitored on a regular basis without the need to anaesthetize and take blood samples.

Whatever the case may be, an interval of 18 months to two years between litters seems to be fairly normal for leopards, though Half-Tail proved the exception to this, lending further credence to Nicholls' and Kat's work. When Beauty was barely ten months old Half-Tail mated again, and three months later gave birth to her fourth litter. By this stage Beauty was already catching small prey such as hares and impala fawns that she found 'lying out' in concealment among the acacia thickets, and like all young leopards she invested considerable time and effort in searching for food. But she was still too young to survive on her own, and for the next few months regularly sought out her mother, feeding from her kills and at times playing and interacting peacefully with her younger brother and sister.

Fritz Polking was able to spend weeks at a time with Half-Tail and her two new two cubs – a male called Mang'aa (Kikuyu for 'the one that doesn't care', in reference to his bold and nonchalant nature) and a female called Taratibu (Swahili for 'pretty') – during this extraordinary period. Although he often saw Beauty with her mother's new family, it was evident that Half-Tail was firmly in control of the situation, snarling and grunting when she wanted her older daughter to keep her distance, ready to intervene if play became too rough, while still holding out a life-line for as long as Beauty needed access to kills. Beauty was even seen to allow the younger cubs to feed from a kill she had made herself.

All cats have the innate ability to stalk, rush and pounce – this is evident whether you are watching a domestic kitten stalking a ball of wool, a cheetah cub creeping up on a bird or a young leopard chasing an agama lizard. What is lacking in the youngsters is the knowledge of which prey is the most suitable to hunt, and how to overpower it once it has been caught – it takes time to learn how to apply an effective killing bite without injuring yourself. This is one reason why young cats remain dependent on their mothers for such a long time. Nevertheless, when it comes to living by their wits and finding a meal, the solitary leopard is a master of the art of killing – in marked contrast to the more social lion. A two-year-old lion is still only a fledgling hunter, and without the help of its pride mates might well starve – it certainly would if it found itself on its own any younger than this. Not so the leopard. By the age of two it will have been independent for a number of months, killing both small and large prey unaided.

Half-Tail inciting Beauty to play with her. She seemed to enjoy play sessions as much as her cubs did.

Just how different the three species of big cats are is highlighted in words I wrote while watching Half-Tail in the early 1990s, when she was still known as the Paradise female:

Within a kilometre of where I sit are eight lions, a mother cheetah accompanied by a year-old cub, and the Paradise female. For the moment all the cats are resting. But how different they are. The Gorge Pride lie sprawled nonchalantly around the base of an acacia bush. Three young cubs wrestle among the giant paws of one of the lionesses, a huge creature. The cubs are relaxed and confident, basking in the powerful presence of their mother. A few hundred metres away, the cheetah female looks constantly about her, responding nervously to the slightest hint of danger, anxious for the safety of the sole survivor of her litter of five cubs. Meanwhile, the leopard, all fluid grace, skulks unseen between them, living out her secret life.

The character and way of life of Africa's three big cats have been moulded by competition for food and living space. Each cat is uniquely suited to its own lifestyle, superbly adapted to catching its prey and surviving among so many other predators. Between them, lions, leopards and cheetahs exhibit the full range of cat behaviour – the heavyweight social cat, the solitary opportunist and the fleet-footed specialist. Together they paint a vivid picture of power and beauty, reminding us why man has deified and worshipped cats in all their many forms since the dawn of time.

Mang'aa (left) and Taratibu, Half-Tail's third litter. Taratibu was killed when she was a year old. Mang'aa survived to maturity and, like most male leopards, moved away from his natal area to seek a territory elsewhere.

Life of a Leopard

While I was trying to follow Chui in the late 1970s and early '80s I made a point of keeping up to date with any articles or photographic essays published on leopards. The work of Bailey and Hamilton had given me an invaluable insight into how many leopards lived in a particular area, the size of their home ranges and how frequently (or infrequently) they made contact with one another. But I had always longed for a more intimate view, a sense of the real animal. It was only when someone happened to mention the existence of a private game sanctuary called Londolozi, in South Africa, that I realized there were other people beginning to watch leopards on a daily basis, gradually piecing together a clearer picture of how these enigmatic creatures live. I was intrigued.

Londolozi is part of the wilderness area known as the Sabi Sand Game Reserve, an association of privately owned game sanctuaries covering an area of 650 km^2 (250 sq. miles) and situated along the western boundary of the Kruger National Park, where Ted Bailey had conducted his leopard research. Many of these properties started life as cattle ranches, and as in the Kruger of the early days their owners took a dim view of predators in every shape and form, applying a ruthless predator-control programme, particularly against lions, hyenas and wild dogs. Leopards and cheetahs felt the brunt of this campaign, too. In those days all predators were considered vermin, to be eradicated to make way for agriculture and livestock ranching. Wilderness was rapidly replaced by large tracts of farmland. Game – as wildlife was commonly called in those days – was either to be eaten, in the case of antelope, or used for financial gain in the form of biltong, hides, ivory and rhino horn. In 1927 Harry Kirkman was employed as warden of the Transvaal Consolidated Land and Exploration Company (TCC), which then owned most of what is today known as the Sabi Sand Complex. The TCC was engaged in cattle-

A Thomson's gazelle carcass hanging from a tree. In the 1970s this was often the only clue I would have to a leopard's presence.

ranching and Kirkman's job was to eradicate predators, particularly lions, that strayed into the area from Kruger. In six years he killed over 400 of them.

Fortunately, attitudes have changed over the intervening decades, to the extent that in 1993 all fences were removed between the Kruger and the Sabi Sand Complex, as well as other similar private reserves such as Timbavati, Klaseries, Umbabat and Manyeleti, allowing the unimpeded movement of game throughout the whole area. An even more visionary approach is now being applied with the creation of TransFrontier parks, huge wilderness areas that have no boundaries. The fence separating Kruger from sanctuaries along the shared border with Mozambique and Zimbabwe is being taken down, allowing the resumption of the traditional east-west migration of species such as zebras, wildebeest and elephants over the whole of this huge natural ecosystem. But the lawlessness currently being witnessed in Zimbabwe has decimated wildlife populations within the country, raising concerns about the long-term viability of such cross-border initiatives.

Meanwhile, the brothers John and Dave Varty, who own Londolozi, had a dream.

They wanted to create a wildlife paradise, to return the land that they had inherited from their father in 1969 to its natural state. Inspired by the work of ecologist Ken Tinley they set about developing the property, which had previously been farmed and hunted, as an ecotourism project. They were going to give the land back to the animals, encouraging tourism through the development of three small luxury camps, and ploughing back some of the revenue into the local community to help them meet their development needs.

In those early days John and Dave took their visitors out in battered old Land-rovers, with a local Shangaan game-tracker seated on the bonnet of the car to search the ground ahead. Once they had located something of interest – rhino, lion, elephant – John or Dave and a tracker would leave the vehicle and set off on foot, armed with a high-powered rifle as back-up. If they were successful in finding what they were searching for they would return to the vehicle and drive closer so that the guests could have the best possible view.

More than anything, it was the chance of seeing a leopard that people wanted – not least the Vartys themselves. They were well aware that Londolozi was ideal leopard country: 130km^2 (50 sq. miles) of dense woodland enveloping a mosaic of open spaces, criss-crossed by dongas – the dry riverbeds with sandy bottoms and dense thickets on their banks where a leopard might give birth to cubs and find cover to hunt. But in those days the leopards were painfully shy.

Today both Londolozi and neighbouring Mala Mala pride themselves on being able to show their guests the 'big five' – lion, leopard, elephant, rhino and buffalo – so revered by trophy hunters. Years of painstakingly tracking generations of leopards from vehicles and on foot have eventually created a population that can be approached at close quarters in a vehicle, which is highly desirable in the thickly bushed environment of the Sabi Sand

Half-Tail and Beauty. Mother leopards are always on the look-out for possible danger – from lions, hyenas or humans on foot.

Reserve. To this day the rangers keep detailed records on the different leopards in their area, building up a comprehensive library of photographs of each individual so that they can recognize them again whenever they are relocated. All sightings and any interesting behaviour are recorded in a game record book. This has enabled the staff to map out the home ranges of individual leopards, and to follow the patterns of dispersal of subadults as they leave their mother and begin to carve out an existence for themselves.

Night game drives have always been particularly popular with visitors to Londolozi. They rely on the skills of the trackers, who sit perched on the rear of the vehicles with a spotlight, throwing an arc of light into the darkness and picking out all manner of nocturnal creatures – tiny Scops owls, genets, bushbabies, civets – that are almost impossible to see during the day. And in the back of everyone's mind in the early days was the hope that they might – just might – have the chance of seeing a leopard. 'Always there but never seen, it moved like a ghost in the night, making its kills, leaving its drag-

marks and footprints and calling hauntingly into the darkness,' was how wildlife photographer Lex Hess described the situation. Hess went to work as a ranger at Londolozi in 1976, but it would be another three years before he could realize his dream of watching and photographing leopards on a regular basis.

That moment came in September 1979, when one of the trackers picked up the glint of two pairs of eyes shining back at him from the topmost branches of a tree, in an area where the tracker and ranger had seen leopard prints earlier in the day. At first they thought the two small spotted creatures must be genets. Then it dawned on them that they were staring into the eyes of two leopard cubs. They could hardly believe their luck. From that day onwards the rangers and trackers carefully pieced together a picture of the mother leopard's movements. Initially she was very shy and they saw little more than her tracks. Every few days she would move her cubs, and each time she did so the rangers and trackers were able to pin down the new location and spend time with the cubs. Gradually the Mother leopard, as she became known, began to relax and within six months she had lost her fear of vehicles. It is thought that she was about three years old when she was first sighted, so it seems likely that the two cubs perched in the tree were her first litter. So began an extraordinary story that helped to establish Londolozi as the place to visit if you wanted the best chance of seeing a leopard.

Not long after this a friend sent me an illustrated article about the leopards at Londolozi. Here was what I had been hoping to record – leopards mating, a mother with cubs, adults fighting – the kind of thing that you just didn't see in the Mara in those days – unless your name was Bwana Chui – let alone photograph. I was able to keep track of events at Londolozi through the newsletter they circulated to friends and clients, giving regular updates on what was happening with their leopards.

By 1991 Lex Hess had managed to collect enough material to publish his magnificent book The Leopards of Londolozi, which documented the story of the Mother leopard and her offspring. The book is a treasure-trove of anecdotes and data, liberally illustrated with Hess's beautiful portraits of the leopard and its world. Much of the behaviour recorded by Hess and the other rangers mirrored what we had been observing in the Mara, first with Chui and the Mara Buffalo female, and then with Half-Tail and her cubs. Similar patterns emerged, reinforcing our ideas of how leopards lived in the wild. But even more exciting were the many insights that were new to Angie and me.

One of the biggest limitations of our work in the Mara has always been that we only watch leopards during the daytime; we never go on night game drives. Even if we were allowed to drive at night it would prove difficult to follow leopards. The Mara's black-cotton soils and haphazard system of tracks do not lend themselves to the tracker's craft, unlike the sandy roads at Londolozi which the leopards often use as convenient travel routes and scent-posts, and which are a great bonus in hunting down these elusive creatures. With the Mara being a National Game Reserve rather than private property one isn't as free to do as one wants, and night game drives in and around the Mara are discouraged. The anti-poaching unit and security personnel have enough on their hands trying to control poaching, without wasting their time worrying about vehicles driving around at night looking for leopards. But just as Hess found at Londolozi, we have discovered leopards are far more active during the day than was previously thought – and this is particularly true of a female with cubs. Eventually we found many opportunities to observe their behaviour during daylight.

In areas where there is plenty of prey, female leopards spend around 80 per cent of their adult lives caring for cubs, and the majority of the rest of their time pregnant. Between 1979 and 1989, the Mother leopard gave birth to nine litters, most of which could be observed from the time they were about two months old. One rarely sees cubs younger than this, so it is almost impossible to know exactly how many cubs are born in each litter, though leopards have been known to have up to six in captivity. In our experience two cubs – occasionally three – seems to be the norm, and five of the Mother leopard's litters numbered two cubs each. Two of her litters had only one cub, and one disappeared before they could be counted or sexed. Of 14 litters known to me in the Mara, only four contained three cubs as far as I could tell – the rest had two. Even if a female gives birth to three cubs, it is rare for her to raise them all to maturity; it may sometimes be that one is a weakling who fails to survive the first few days. As far as is known the Mother leopard produced only one litter of three cubs during this period, and when she did, two of them were killed by lions when they were about four months old.

Leopards give birth at any time of the year, though there is some evidence to show that in certain areas they breed seasonally. Situated astride the Equator, Kenya experiences two wet and two dry seasons each year. This is a different weather pattern from southern Africa, where there are just two distinct seasons – a dry winter from April to October, and a wet summer from November to March. Many southern African birds and mammals give birth in midsummer, between December and February. Bailey's data from Kruger appears to point to a peak in leopards mating and giving birth, though this is based on observation of only six litters. He found that most courtship occurred during the late dry season from July to September (49 per cent), coinciding with the greatest concentration of impalas; only 9 per cent occurred in the wet season, from January to March. The peak in mating obviously produced a peak in leopard

A mother leopard with three cubs aged about six to eight weeks. All three survived to independence, a significant achievement in the Mara.

births some three months later, between October and December/January. This meant that more cubs were born during the early wet season than at any other period, matching the pattern of impala births. Five of the six leopard litters observed were born during the early wet season, and three of these were in December. At this time there is plenty of good cover – vital for a mother with tiny cubs – and the young impala are easy to catch and ideal for bringing back to the place where she has left small cubs. More leopards died and showed poor condition during the dry season, suggesting that hunting was more difficult at this time of the year when there was the least cover to help them in stalking their prey.

Bailey recorded no leopard births in the winter months, which tallies with the more recent findings of wildlife filmmakers Dale Hancock and Kim Wolhuter in the adjoining Mala Mala reserve. All seven litters produced during their filming were born between September and February. But if this does point to a significant peak in breeding, how is such a thing brought about? Would a leopard's lower nutritional levels and poorer body condition mean she had less chance of becoming pregnant if

the season wasn't right? Might she even abort or miscarry her foetuses?

In the Mara I have recorded 14 litters of cubs from five females. Cubs were born in every month except February, March and May, but most leopards gave birth in the long dry season of July to October, and at the beginning of the short rainy season that lasts from mid-October to December. Only one litter was recorded in the long rainy season from March to the end of May. It certainly seems to benefit a leopard female if her cubs are born around the time of the short rains, as this is when many of the prey animals also have their young, and a mother leopard often targets warthog piglets and impala calves during this period. This is also the time when the wildebeest and zebra migration is in the Mara, ensuring that there is plenty of food for the hyenas and lions, helping to reduce competition for the smaller prey that leopards hunt.

Scientists working with the Serengeti Lion Project have noted a seasonal peak in breeding and in births, which is thought to be tied to the lionesses' nutritional state and related to the movements of one of their main prey species – the wildebeest. Though lionesses give birth at any time of

Half-Tail hauling a freshly killed impala into the safety of a fig tree. Her daughter Zawadi had been feeding on the ground until hyenas began to arrive.

when the migration is in the area. There may be a similar peak in the Mara coinciding with the period when the migration is in the northern part of the ecosystem – June to October.

In Londolozi, Hess found that all the leopard females he observed became very secretive just before giving birth, seeking out places that are either hidden from view or particularly secure, such as a cave or crevices in a rocky outcrop or overhang, or in a dense thicket. A termite mound covered with vegetation, the depression

the year, there is a peak in the Serengeti between March and July. This may be partly because when the wildebeest return to the Serengeti in November and December there is an upsurge in pride takeovers due to the influx of nomadic males that follow

the herds. Lionesses also tend to reach peak physical condition during this period because food is abundant, and this prompts them to come into season more often, regardless of pride takeovers. Hence most pregnancies or suckling of small cubs occur

Plains zebras congregating at a waterhole during the dry season. When there is little moisture in the grass, wildebeest and zebras must drink almost daily.

beneath a hollow fallen log or the holes in the roots of a tree were also popular hiding places – anywhere, in fact, that a cub can crawl into when its mother departs. In the Kalahari leopard cubs are often born in aardvark burrows, and stay there or under bushes during their mother's absence; adults also use burrows as daytime resting places as a way of avoiding the Kalahari's intense heat. Just how important a secure hiding place is was illustrated when a hyena came sniffing around the hollow base of a tree where a mother leopard had hidden her young cub. The hyena was unable to extricate the cub, which spat and hissed in defiance. Eventually the hyena moved off.

One fortunate group of visitors to Leopard Gorge witnessed Half-Tail's daughter Zawadi giving birth to her third litter in 2001, by which time Safi, the only survivor of her previous litter, was nearly two years old. Guided by Shieni Ropiara from Kichwa Tembo Camp, George McKnight and Christine Hart were with two other couples on a morning game drive and had already enjoyed dawn encounters with elephants and lions. But what happened at around midday on 28 September was a once-in-a-lifetime experience for all of them. Shieni had heard over his radio that Zawadi had been seen in the area, and as Christine wrote:

Shieni knew the most likely lair and positioned our vehicle on the bank

Wildebeest leaving the plains and heading for one of the river-crossing sites along the Mara River.

Zawadi with a three-week-old cub in Leopard Gorge. She has produced nine cubs in all, of which only one – Safi – has survived.

Like all cats, mother leopards carry cubs in their mouth up to the time that they are about eight weeks old. Young cubs have dark coats with tightly packed spots.

Zawadi suckling Safi and her brother along Fig Tree Ridge – her second litter of cubs.

opposite two boulders which framed the entrance. From a distance of about 25m (80ft), we were able to look downwards into the small cave and get our first glimpse of Zawadi…. As we watched through binoculars and marvelled at her beauty, Zawadi got up, turned around and became more visible. Then to our astonishment she began to give birth. As the sac emerged she doubled round to help it out, and we watched spellbound as she worked to free the cub. About 20 minutes later the procedure was repeated, though this time Zawadi, possibly aware that she had an audience, moved so the delivery of the second cub was not so clearly seen. But the post-natal attention and the subsequent release of the cub were well observed.

Though Zawadi remained at the gorge for the next month, no-one saw the cubs again, and she eventually left the area. The cubs can't have survived, because three and a half months later she was seen mating in the gorge, though this time she failed to become pregnant. Not until the following August – eleven months after she had been seen giving birth – did she produce another litter. Once again she chose the gorge as their birthplace.

For the first few days after her cubs are born a mother leopard spends the majority of her time with them, providing them with warmth and milk. When she does go hunting she remains very localized in her movements, returning every few hours to suckle the cubs, and every so often transfer them to a new location, sometimes no more than 100m (330ft) away, often less. We watched Zawadi move her fourth litter eight times in two weeks as she worked her way from one end of Leopard Gorge to the other – a distance of no more than 300m (1,000ft). At Londolozi the longest time a mother spent with young cubs at the same den was 16 days, prior to which she moved them every five days on average. But as we had seen with Chui and her mother years earlier, leopards adapt their behaviour to suit local conditions, and if they feel secure at one particular location they may stay there for months.

Zawadi lost two of that fourth litter during her stay in the gorge, and when she moved the third cub, then aged about four weeks, to a new area we were fascinated to see where her new hiding place might be. She travelled a total of 6km (4 miles) due north, carrying the cub in her mouth and eventually hiding it among the roots of a fallen tree on a rocky hillside known as Moses Rock. This was the same area that we had often found her with her daughter Safi the previous year, and the same area that her mother Half-Tail had used in 1998 when rearing her sixth and final litter.

Moses Rock is an ideal location, with lots of trees and thickets as well as jumbles of rock that make a series of nooks and crannies in which to hide small cubs. When a fire set by Masai pastoralists rampaged through the area in September 2002, we were concerned that Zawadi's cub might perish, but fortunately the fire burned around the fallen tree, and as it turned out Zawadi had already moved the youngster to a cluster of rocks higher up the hillside.

Some time later I explored Moses Rock on foot, and had a chance to see exactly where Zawadi had hidden her cub. Beneath the fallen tree were a number of small passageways among the decaying roots and jumble of rocks, just big enough for a cub to crawl into. Zawadi used to leave the cub while she went off hunting, calling whenever she returned with a guttural arragh-grunt or by making a puffing sound, and soon enough the cub would emerge from its hiding place to suckle and be groomed. The second lair was a cub-sized crevice among rocks which became progressively narrower, making it almost impossible for a predator to extract a cub, though a venomous snake such as a puff

adder might have been able to enter and aim a deadly strike at it. Though I had always thought of Leopard Gorge and Fig Tree Ridge as ideal birthplaces, it was evident that there were many other areas offering a multitude of safe retreats, even though they were nothing like as photogenic – in fact they were a nightmare for anyone hoping to photograph a leopard with cubs. But then no doubt a leopard would like that.

Africa's three big cats adopt different strategies to minimize the risk to their young offspring – particularly in a place such as the Mara where there are so many predators. A cheetah mother must defend and feed her cubs on her own, just like a leopard – but the similarities end there. Cheetahs generally range over such large areas in their search for prey that cubs begin to follow their mother as soon as they are six to seven weeks old, and from then on remain with her; their rapidly maturing mobility is adapted to this requirement, which allows the mother the freedom to hunt wherever prey is most easily available. This is vital in the Serengeti and parts of the Mara, where a cheetah's main prey is the Thomson's gazelle – a migratory species. To keep track of the gazelles' movements a mother cheetah may have to undertake lengthy journeys, so life becomes far easier once her cubs can follow. In fact she may even abandon small cubs when they are still at a den if she is forced to commute too far – with a gestation period of just three months, it is better for her to try again when conditions may be more favourable.

Many cheetah cubs don't survive the first few months, which is no doubt why cheetahs produce larger litters than the other big cats – five or more is not unusual. In the 1980s scientists in the Serengeti became concerned about reports that litter sizes seemed to be diminishing, and wondered if this might be a consequence of low levels of genetic diversity – Africa's cheetah population is very inbred. What

they found instead was that cheetah cubs are highly vulnerable to predation, and that only 5 per cent reach maturity in places like the Serengeti, where lions and hyenas are responsible for 70 per cent of the losses.

When a mother cheetah hunts, young cubs tend to sit and watch, waiting for her to bring a gazelle or impala fawn back to them or to call them with that high-pitched, bird-like whistle that carries across the plains and prompts them to rush towards her, eager to begin feeding. If danger threatens in the form of lions or hyenas a cheetah's only choice is to try and distract these larger predators, rushing towards them growling and hissing, slapping at the ground with her forepaws, hair bristling, teeth bared, veering off only when she is almost on top of them and using her greater speed to try to lead them away while the cubs escape.

Meanwhile, lion cubs are able to enjoy the benefits of the pride system. By being raised as part of a crèche, they are provided with the best start in life – suckled, fed and protected communally by the lionesses. Once they are old enough to be introduced to the rest of the pride – at around eight weeks – they can be brought into the open and led to wherever a kill has been made. Thereafter they spend much of their time with other members of the pride. Though lionesses often leave their cubs among cover when they go off hunting, this proves increasingly difficult once the cubs are six to nine months old. By that age they often insist on following along behind the lionesses as they move about, and sometimes try to stalk up on prey – in the process ruining many a hunting opportunity for the adults, but gaining valuable practice in how, when and what to hunt. Lion cubs tend to rest together – as do cheetahs – and the close bonds that they establish with siblings of a similar age is vital to their well-being as adults, forging relationships that bind groups of males and groups of females together for life.

Leopards take a much more furtive approach to raising their cubs, shielding them from view during the first few months and then leaving them to their own devices for much of the time.

Like all young cats, leopard cubs are very inquisitive. They are attracted by movement, and from the earliest age will stalk and pounce. It is difficult to ascertain how much they gain from watching their mother, as she often hunts alone and needs to remain hidden from view to creep close to her prey. But she will sometimes bring small creatures that are not yet dead back to the cubs, allowing them to practise a killing bite. If there is more than one cub they will play together for hours at a time, and many of their games revolve around behaviour patterns that they will need to have mastered by the time they become independent – stalking, pouncing, biting, fighting, escaping from attack and learning to deal with the complexities of how to kill various animals. Nonetheless, cubs frequently seek out their own resting places from an early age, as if they prefer their own company – a way of being that typifies all leopards.

One cub is often dominant over the other, either because one is a male and with age becomes bigger and stronger, or simply because one is tougher in temperament. Regardless of this, leopards retain their curiosity for the first two years of life and remain very cubbish and playful in character. But once they settle down and have cubs of their own or have to defend a territory, life seems to take on a more serious aspect and they may abandon their relaxed demeanour.

Thomson's gazelles are the cheetah's main prey in the Mara–Serengeti.

Because so much of what leopards do is hidden from view it is hard to gauge at what age they make their first kills, though in general it seems to be at around six to nine months. Occasionally a leopard may

A mother cheetah must be constantly vigilant due to the threat posed to her cubs and herself by other predators.
Cheetahs regularly use termite mounds as vantage points to look for prey or keep an eye out for danger.

Six-week-old lion cubs from the Marsh Pride. At this age a lioness usually keeps her cubs hidden, introducing them to the rest of the pride when they are eight weeks old.

have the opportunity to kill earlier than this – we witnessed a three-month-old male cub of Zawadi's sneak into a crevice along Fig Tree Ridge and emerge with a young hyrax while on a walkabout with his mother and sister. A day or so after this we saw Zawadi patiently stalk a hare that was crouched motionless among a tangle of vegetation beneath a fallen acacia bush. When she was close enough, she darted forward and pounced on it, grabbing it by the neck. Instead of killing it she carefully carried it back along the top of the ridge to where she had left the cubs, then dropped it – still alive – in front of them. They immediately grabbed it and mauled it before launching into a brief but vicious

tussle over possession, which the slightly larger male won. When young cubs fight like this their mother is quick to intervene, biting down on them until they stop squabbling, or snatching the kill away and repositioning it in a tree. Apart from playing the role of peacemaker and preventing her cubs from injuring one another, she may also be anxious to stifle the noise the youngsters are making, which might attract the unwanted attention of other predators.

Despite the need to remain concealed, a mother leopard will at times encourage her cubs to take the initiative. Hess watched a female leading her offspring to a burrow where warthogs had taken refuge, and then

hold back as the cubs tried to kill the piglets. On another occasion a mother leopard caught an adult impala by the hindquarters and let her cub jump onto it before releasing it. The antelope immediately shook itself free and bounded away, leaving the cub looking perplexed and causing the mother to rush after the impala and dispatch it with a throat-hold. Once the impala was dead the cub stalked, pounced and then bit it in the throat. It is apparent from these observations how vital this period of trial and error is in allowing cubs the chance to refine their hunting and killing skills. Without their mother there to intervene, they could easily be hurt or fail to find food. Even so, the fledgling hunters

Zawadi pouncing on a hare she has surprised among a tangle of grass. Female and subadult leopards invest considerable time searching for small prey such as this.

do not always have things their own way. A banded mongoose managed to save its life by biting a cub that attacked it, forcing the predator onto the defensive and giving itself time to escape.

By one year of age a leopard has its full complement of permanent teeth, though the canines do not reach their maximum length until they are a year and a half to two years old. This may have some bearing on when they become able to kill larger prey. Full independence often seems to coincide with this transition, though as we have seen the arrival of a new litter of cubs may be the main factor in finally terminating contact between a mother and her young, and Beauty was killing full-grown Thomson's gazelles by the time she was a year old.

At Mala Mala a young male known as the Mlowathi male gained independence from his mother at around 14 months. Not long after this he was observed attacking a full-grown male warthog, struggling to subdue it for 25 minutes in a noisy battle as he vainly tried to transfer his hold from the pig's head to its throat. The pig was too big

for the leopard to drag into a tree and inevitably its blood-curdling squeals attracted a pride of nine lions, forcing the smaller cat to flee for his life. At around the same time he managed to find and kill a bushbuck fawn, biting it in the head. Male cubs are substantially bigger and stronger than their sisters by this age, allowing them

to catch and overpower larger prey. Hess mentions an eleven-month-old male killing a young male impala and using the throat-hold expertly. By this age he was also attempting to kill warthog piglets and was quick to learn that mother pigs will bravely defend their young against predators the size of leopards and cheetahs.

Young leopards often chase vervet monkeys from tree to tree, something that adult leopards generally do not bother doing, though I once saw Half-Tail eating a vervet that she had killed. The young female at Mala Mala on whom Dale Hancock and Kim Wolhuter focused most of their attention was particularly quick and adept at harassing vervets, intimidating them to the point where they would freeze in terror and cling trembling to the branches, unable to move. Tjellers, as she was known, would then catch one with little effort, plucking it from the tree and worrying it in a mock attack, but never killing it. By contrast a young male in the same reserve, known as the Hogvaal male, tended to target far larger prey. Full of the exuberance of youth, coupled with the added size, strength and boldness that characterize male leopards, he stalked giraffe, adult kudu and wildebeest – even

Zawadi carrying a live hare back to her three-month-old cubs, allowing them the chance to practise their hunting skills on it.

*A*mong the more obvious targets for young leopards are small prey such as mice, hares, mongooses, francolins – creatures that are easy to overpower and unlikely to injure them. One male cub at Londolozi killed a full-grown civet weighing 10kg (22lb) when he was eight months old and weighed about 15–20kg (33–44lb), and then played with it but did not eat it. In the next three weeks he and his sister killed a monkey, a banded mongoose, a scrub hare and a francolin, kills that their mother's previous litters had not started to make until they were between nine and eleven months. Small prey such as this is often dispatched with a bite to the head or neck, which is typical of the way small cats kill; there is no need to apply the bite to the throat favoured by all three big cats. Lions sometimes use a suffocating hold over the nose and mouth when the prey is a really large animal such as a buffalo, and a female leopard attacking a topi cow with a broken leg – far bigger prey than she would have attempted to kill had the antelope been healthy – used a similar hold, but the topi managed to struggle free and escape.

Zawadi and Safi in 2000. Safi was nearly one year old at the time and had killed (and partially eaten) a white tailed mongoose.

regularly trying his luck with a herd of buffaloes that would quickly turn on him and force him to seek refuge in the nearest tree. Not content with making kills the size of a young zebra, he attacked an adult kudu, jumping on to its back like a lion hunting a buffalo, and forcing the antelope to collapse under his weight.

The road to independence exacts a heavy price, and the mortality rate for subadult leopards is nearly twice that of adults. Not only does it take time for hunting skills to be refined, but to breed successfully a leopard must establish a territory of its own. In areas such as the Mara–Serengeti and the Kruger good leopard habitat is going to be occupied, and the best hunting grounds are liable to be aggressively defended by resident adults. Under such competitive conditions a young leopard could easily find itself having to fight for a permanent home or to remain in a less productive area, where the chances of finding food and mating opportunities were greatly reduced. Hardly surprisingly, quite a number of young and old or injured leopards either die of starvation or are forced into taking livestock or killing dogs around settlements, and are shot or poisoned in retaliation.

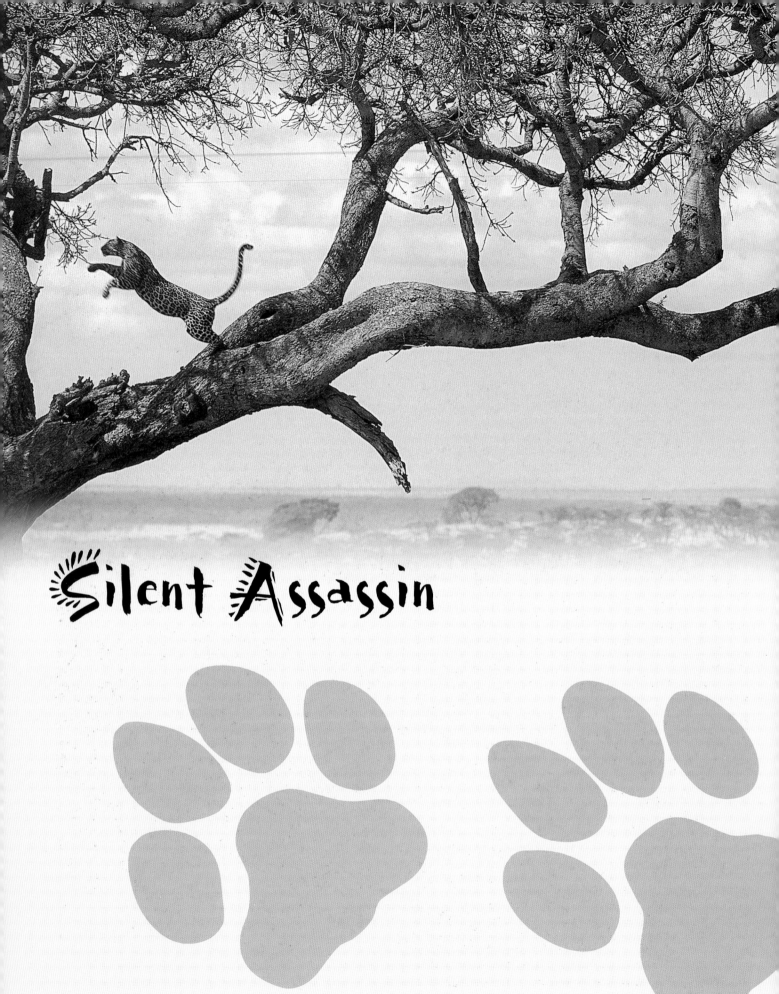

Silent Assassin

Leopards are the quintessential stalking cat, creeping closer to their prey than lions or cheetahs would ever attempt. The cheetah hunts in the open and has the blinding burst of speed that allows it to run down its prey; the lion is a stalker but targets larger prey that is generally slower off the mark than an impala or gazelle, and will continue to pursue its quarry in open country if it feels there is a chance of overhauling it in the first few hundred metres. But a leopard cannot afford to hunt in the open where it might be caught out by lions or hyenas. It is a creature of the thickets and forests, bounding forward and overpowering its victim only when it is almost on top of it. A leopard will always stalk that extra metre rather than launching itself forward and missing its prey. Stealth – and a quiet kill – are essential if it isn't to attract unwanted attention from its larger competitors. This is why a leopard moves away quickly once it has been seen and the alarm calls are ringing in its ears, signalling to all and sundry that a predator is about.

Dale Hancock and Kim Wolhuter followed leopards at Mala Mala day and night for several years – Wolhuter is now a permanent resident – and Hancock wrote a book about their experiences. They soon discovered that although Tjellers, in typical cat fashion, rested for much of the time, she adopted a fairly predictable routine at night, with three peaks in activity. When she had a kill safely stashed in a tree she tended to stay in the vicinity until it was finished, alternating rest periods in the tree or on the ground with bouts of feeding and grooming, though she sometimes went to drink at the nearest source of water. This was similar to the routine that Zawadi adopted when she had a kill. At other times Tjellers would generally start hunting at sunset and continue for a few hours until about 10 p.m., after which she would rest wherever she was until around 1 a.m. Then she would move off again and continue prowling. If she were still unsuccessful she would rest for a few hours until just before first light, and then try one more time. This dawn patrol often lasted for as long as it remained cool enough to move about comfortably. During the winter when the weather was cool and dry, and Tjellers was

Half-Tail watching a female impala, having already ambushed her fawn 'lying out' in a thicket and carried it into the acacia bush.

To watch a leopard hunting is sublime, a mixture of grace, suppleness and power, using sight, hearing and smell to track their prey. They will sit and listen, sniff the air, perhaps climbing into a tree or onto a termite mound for a better view of their surroundings. Occasionally they will abandon their cautious, methodical approach and run like a cheetah in a fast sprint to overhaul an easy target such as an impala fawn or warthog piglet. They may even sit up on their haunches mongoose-style to peer over the long grass, something that you never see a lion or cheetah doing, probably because leopards spend much more of their time in dense cover than lions or cheetahs. Though cats do not have such an acute sense of smell as wild dogs, jackals or hyenas, they are quite capable of following the scent trails left by prey – or other leopards, or their enemies. Camouflage and patience are precious advantages. A leopard will watch the direction in which its prey is moving and then circle ahead to intercept it, often lying in wait, adjusting its position where necessary; a deadly game of hide and seek. It may stalk, be seen, move away and then stalk the same prey all over again. A stalk of an hour or more is not unusual, with a leopard sometimes noting the direction of prey from a vantage point in a tree or from a ridge top, and only later moving off in that direction, sniffing the ground, picking up the sounds of its quarry and monitoring its route as it heads off in pursuit.*

Chui stalking impalas. Leopards use every available patch of cover to creep closer to their prey, and where cover is sparse they can always wait until dark.

really determined to find food, she might remain active until midday. If she was nursing cubs, she often returned to them during rest periods.

With small prey such as grass rats, I have seen Half-Tail and Zawadi perform an agile, high-arching pounce like a serval or jackal, landing with forepaws right on top of the victim concealed in the grass. And there is no craftier cat to meet the challenge of crossing open terrain, flattening itself against the ground, legs bent beneath it, snaking forward, then disappearing into a lugga for concealment, peering from behind a termite mound or even using a vehicle to screen itself from view. Lex Hess watched one leopard chase a herd of impala in the open, driving them towards the cover of a thicket. Finding themselves blocked by a wall of bush, some of the impalas turned back, straight into the outstretched paws of the leopard. Who knows if this was strategy or opportunism?

Leopards are known for their predilection for dogs – domestic and wild – and they can be the bane of a dog-lover's life, sneaking around villages at night and waylaying any dog that is foolish enough to think it is safe to close its eyes. Nothing is too big or too small when it comes to hunting down a dog – or a cat, for that matter. Many years ago, when we were living at Kichwa Tembo camp, a leopard was seen trotting off with Esmerelda, our favourite domestic cat, in its mouth. A reputation for fierceness means nothing to a leopard, as a priest living in the Mara region discovered when his full-grown rottweiler was taken by a leopard without uttering a sound. More recently, our Nairobi neighbours Frank and Dolcie Howitt had the tranquillity of an evening stroll shattered when a leopard burst from a bush and snatched one of their dogs, a Jack Russell terrier. But it takes more than a leopard to keep Frank and Dolcie from their walk, and besides, they presumed that the leopard was just passing through. A day or so later, however, it struck again. This time, Frank, who is built like a solid English oak, managed to scare it off, leaving one terrified labrador in need of a patchwork of stitches. The leopard was later trapped and moved by the Kenya Wildlife Service.

Among wild canids, jackals feature regularly on the list of species killed by leopards, which is no doubt the reason why these foxy creatures act with such alarm at the sight or smell of the big cat. In fact black-backed jackals can be a real pest for a leopard, while bringing joy to leopard enthusiasts such as ourselves, uttering incessant, high-pitched barks the minute they see our spotted friend, and in the process pointing us in the right direction. Zawadi would sometimes show her irritation when mobbed by jackals, appearing as if she wanted to trick them into coming just a little closer. Every prey animal knows its 'flight distance' – how close it is safe to approach, based on its ability to turn and outrun a predator if necessary. Zawadi would suddenly lie down and roll on her back, almost playfully, enticing the jackals to come closer, then spring to her feet and chase after them at a fast gallop. But jackals are almost as crafty as leopards, and can dart and jink with incredible agility, though they do miscalculate at times and end up in the leopard's jaws. When they establish a den in a termite mound, as they tend to do each September in the Mara, they are particularly wary of revealing their hiding place to a leopard, and have even more reason to want to escort it off the property.

Even guinea fowl will race after a leopard among the acacia thickets, looking like motorized tea-cosies, clucking and churring in alarm. The leopard knows that the game is up and quickly finds a new place to conceal itself.

In the olden days, artists often depicted a leopard ambushing its prey from the concealment of a tree, leaping from the branches directly onto its victim. Though this rarely happens, filmmaker Richard Matthews did manage to capture just such a sequence in the Mara in 1985, when a female leopard jumped onto the back of a zebra foal and then killed it. Normally a leopard that spots potential prey from a tree quickly descends and then stalks or runs to get into a good position to ambush it. From the ground it has far more options in responding to what the prey might do,

Beauty leaping from a tree after being chased and harassed by a male cheetah.

and it must be rare for a leopard to find itself in a position to jump directly onto prey from a tree-top, though it may leap to the ground and then pounce. The slightest movement in the tree is likely to give a split-second warning to the prey, which is usually capable of outdistancing a leopard.

Subadult leopards, and sometimes adult females, invest a considerable amount of energy in stalking small prey– particularly hares and hyrax – as they move about their territory, and will target the young of many species, including impala fawns, warthog piglets and wildebeest calves. Females of larger species such as wildebeest and topi will defend their young from attack by hyenas, wild dogs, cheetahs and leopards, something they wouldn't risk doing with lions. Angie and I once witnessed Half-Tail

launch a lightning attack on a two-month-old wildebeest calf that had been born months after the peak calving season in the Serengeti, making it an obvious target (most wildebeest calves are born within a few weeks of each other, providing a glut of prey for the predators but giving an individual, protected by the vast numbers of the herds, the best chance of survival). The cow wildebeest was running through the acacia thickets along the top of Fig Tree Ridge with her calf pressed close to her side, not far from where Half-Tail had left her cubs. Half-Tail grabbed the calf, prompting the mother to turn and charge her. But Half-Tail was too quick and experienced, summoning all her considerable strength to hoist herself and the calf into the nearest bush. The cow flailed away at the bush with her sharp, curved horns, but to no avail, and she soon gave up and ran off, leaving Half-Tail to drag the calf to one of the fig trees, providing food for her and the cubs for the next two or three days.

Adult warthogs are even more dangerous than an irate wildebeest mother, though all the big cats prey heavily on warthog piglets and sometimes lie in ambush at the entrance of a burrow waiting for the pigs to leave or enter. Leopards have even been observed entering a burrow and dragging a piglet out, and Half-Tail was once seen catching three piglets at a burrow. Having eaten two of them she set off for where young Zawadi was waiting along Fig Tree Ridge, carrying

the third piglet in her mouth. But she never got that far. A hyena forced her to seek shelter in a tree, where the temptation to eat the pig herself was too much for her. A mother warthog will invariably challenge a leopard if her piglets are attacked, whipping round and charging the predator, sometimes thumping into it and bowling it over, slashing with her razor-sharp lower tusks. Many a leopard has been forced to drop the piglet and flee to save itself from injury. Even lions have received gaping wounds from an altercation with a large warthog, though the pig usually ends up being overpowered and killed, particularly if a second lion arrives on the scene.

Leopards often bite small prey such as young warthogs in the back of the neck or

head. But when they target larger animals, many of which – such as impalas and Thomson's gazelles – have sharp horns, they have to adopt the easiest way of overpowering prey with the least risk of injury, avoiding the horns and flailing hooves by pinning the animal to the ground with a bite to the throat. This technique employs the leopard's long canines to good effect, sometimes hastening death through loss of blood as well as strangulation. In Londolozi three-quarters of the leopards' prey is made up of just three species: impalas, duikers and warthogs, with the majority of kills being impalas, the most abundant large mammal in the area. Monkeys, bushbucks and hares are also regularly taken, and smaller prey

Half-Tail carrying a wildebeest calf to the safety of a fig tree. A kill of this size would normally last her for two or three days.

Wildebeest watching Zawadi, who is signalling by her posture and the way she is arching her tail that she is not hunting.

Half-Tail with a warthog piglet. All the large predators in the Mara kill warthog piglets, which are born in September/October, at the beginning of the short rains.

includes mice, tree squirrels, spring hares, rock monitors, leopard tortoises and birds, with francolins, red-billed wood hoopoes, hornbills, quails and korhaans featuring among them. One young leopard in the Mara killed a succession of white storks, 'naïve' winter migrants from Eastern Europe, taking six in a ten-day period and carefully plucking them before eating.

This wide range of prey underlines what a versatile and opportunistic hunter the leopard is, far more so than lions or cheetahs. The majority of their kills weigh less than 50kg (110lb), though they have been known to kill animals far in excess of their own weight. On one occasion Half-Tail, who weighed about 40kg (90lb), killed a full-grown Coke's hartebeest weighing 125kg (275lb), and a male leopard in the Mara attacked an adult bull wildebeest with a broken leg. It weighed about 225kg (500lb) and the leopard suffocated it only

after a long struggle. But kills as large as this are unusual, particularly in areas where there are lots of other predators that might steal the leopard's meal.

In fact there is little that a leopard won't kill when it is hungry – one large male at Lewa Wildlife Conservancy in Kenya is known to have killed a month-old rhino calf and stored it in a fig tree. Not even snakes are immune. A leopard at Mala Mala was seen playing a crafty game with a python, having been attracted by the distress calls of a duiker the snake had just caught. The leopard watched as the python coiled itself around its victim and suffocated it. When the leopard approached, the python struck out aggressively and the cat backed off. But as soon as the python had swallowed the duiker, the leopard walked up and clouted the snake on the head, forcing it to disgorge its prey, with which the leopard promptly ran away.

Crocodiles are quite a different proposition and have been known to leave the safety of the river to steal a leopard's kill; even lions sometimes lose kills to crocodiles when the wildebeest and zebra cross the Mara River, ending up in a tug of war with one or more crocodiles. Crocodiles are known to have killed and eaten adult leopards that ventured into the water, though a leopard will kill a small crocodile for food. They may even fish for their supper, snagging catfish from shallow water with their claws, something that Angie and I witnessed a young lioness doing in the Okavango Delta in Botswana.

Though the leopard is a consummate predator, superbly adapted to a killing way of life, it too has to face the threat of predation. Many leopard cubs die before they are a year old, particularly in areas where leopards, lions and hyenas occur together. Cubs that are too small – or too

Safi at three months, seeking refuge in a dead tree. The ability to climb trees from an early age is often the difference between life and death for leopard cubs when confronted by lions or hyenas.

nocturnal, but leopards are also quite often active during the daytime when most lions and hyenas have sought shade and are sleeping or resting.

Of all the leopard's competitors, hyenas probably have the greatest impact in terms of food, certainly in the Mara. Hyenas are so adaptable and have such remarkable senses of smell and hearing that they are often able to steal food from a leopard before it can get a carcass into a tree. Although they generally kill larger prey, they also take young and sometimes adult impalas and gazelles – two of the leopard's most important food sources. Hyenas will seek out young leopards and kill them if they are not well protected in the first few months of their life, but they rarely attack healthy adults.

A Marsh lioness stalking. Lions kill leopards of all ages, hunting them down whenever they get the chance.

slow – to climb trees are often unable to take other evasive action. Mortality in Londolozi and Mala Mala averaged 50–60 per cent, and in the Mara, which has one of the highest densities of lions and hyenas in Africa – one lion per 3 km² (1.1 sq. miles) and one hyena per km² (⅓ sq. mile) – the survival rate is even lower. Half-Tail and Zawadi both lost 80 per cent of their cubs.

All of the large predators compete with one another for food, though competition is reduced by the fact that lions tend to take larger prey than leopards, killing adult wildebeest, zebras and buffaloes, while leopards generally take only the young of these species and prefer medium-sized ungulates such as impalas and gazelles. Both lions and leopards are primarily

Lions, on the other hand, are more likely to kill leopards than to deprive them of much food; although they will certainly attempt to steal a leopard's kill if they spot it wedged in a tree that is easy to climb, they mostly fail to detect a well-concealed larder. Lions rarely eat other predators that they have killed, though one pride did take a small portion of meat from the carcass of an adult male leopard they ambushed in the Mara. The leopard had fled in panic out of a tree after being surrounded by tourist vehicles, and charged straight at the lions. Cornered, it never had any hope of escape;

it was promptly overpowered and strangled.

Half-Tail almost lost her life to lions while preoccupied with eating a hare on the ground. Alerted to the possibility of a meal by the strident alarm calls of a pair of jackals, two lionesses left the shade of a croton thicket where they had been resting and ran to investigate. The moment the lionesses saw Half-Tail crouched over her kill, they began to stalk her. Fortunately the leopard saw them at the last moment and bounded into the topmost branches of a sturdy fig tree, where she devoured the rest of her kill, with barely a glance towards her adversaries. Such incidents must be commonplace to a leopard, for whom keeping out of trouble is a way of life.

Rangers at Londolozi and Mala Mala witnessed lions killing leopard cubs on a number of occasions. In one incident a group of lions picked up the scent of where a mother leopard had left her offspring hidden in a donga. They immediately veered off and surprised the youngsters, with a young male leading the chase. Though one of the cubs managed to escape into the bush, the other was too slow and was caught. With a growl the male lion bit the cub, then shook it several times before dropping it on the ground and biting it again. The other lions rushed to the scene and took it in turns to bite and shake the cub, before moving off to investigate the scent of a dead impala that the Mother leopard had killed.

Lions are bullies and they deal with leopards as ruthlessly as they would an adversary of their own or any other species. Wild dogs are particularly vulnerable, especially when a pack is moving through bush country with young puppies and is easy to ambush, with the lions killing as many of their smaller opponents as they can. Male lions seem even more belligerent towards other predators than lionesses, partly perhaps because they are so much larger and can more easily intimidate rivals, and also because they rely on scavenging from kills made by lionesses or by stealing

Beauty snarling with displeasure, having been chased into a tree by a male cheetah.
Sometimes a leopard is forced to sit up in a tree all day after fleeing from lions.

from other predators. Though lionesses do kill hyenas, leopards and cheetahs at times, they don't seem to have quite the same unforgiving streak as males.

Leopards are far more unpredictable and volatile than lions. Dale Hancock found that at Mala Mala a leopard would let a human pass close by, crouching concealed in the grass, but if the person happened to notice the leopard it might prompt an immediate charge. Lions confronted by a human on foot tend to mock-charge; if you hold your ground they will normally back off. Leopards will charge, and then charge again, forcing you to give ground. Under such frightening circumstances there seems to be some disagreement as to whether to make or avoid eye contact. In a cat's world staring is an act of aggression, averting your eyes an act of submission. Most people would agree that backing off – rather than turning and running – is the best option, though your legs may say otherwise.

There have been instances when a leopard has been so quick and agile that it managed to escape when challenged by a lion, squirming free from beneath the larger adversary. On another occasion a leopard charged a lioness, pulling up only a metre or so from her face, hissing defensively. The lioness was so surprised by this gutsy display that she backed off, and the leopard was able to flee. Small, fierce creatures can be frightening, particularly members of the cat family with their repertoire of explosive spits and coughs. There is no doubt that a cat's dagger-like canines and razor-sharp claws are reason enough not to fight unnecessarily, regardless of the size of your opponent. Nonetheless, lions normally manage to put the fear of God into a leopard, causing it to empty its bladder with the stress of confrontation even when safely perched in the top of a tree. In fact a leopard has only to hear lions roaring nearby to make a hasty retreat, and if it

picks up their scent it sniffs the ground, carefully examining the spot, then moves away in the opposite direction.

Fortunately for leopards, lions are far clumsier climbers, though in one incident a lioness pursued a leopard cub into a tree, prompting the terrified youngster to fall to the ground where it was mauled to death by a second lioness. Half-Tail's daughter Taratibu was killed by a lioness when she was a year old, although her mother and brother escaped into the trees.

The response of a mother leopard on finding a dead cub is the same as we have witnessed with a lioness. She sniffs at it, licking and grooming it briefly before picking it up and carrying it around. Then she settles down to feed on the lifeless body, sometimes storing her grizzly find in a tree. Every so often she calls, using both the short, abrupt, rather guttural arragh-grunt that mother leopards use to summon their cubs from their hiding place, as well as

Hyenas have acute hearing and sense of smell, and keep a watchful eye on vulture activity, which helps lead them to kills made by other predators.

the more robust and far-carrying contact call that all adults employ to let others know of their whereabouts. This process of wandering and calling may go on for a number of days, occasionally up to a week. This is not as pointless as it might seem. A mother leopard often leaves her cubs on their own for days at a time, and sometimes they move away from their hiding place. Under these circumstances, calling and searching have survival value.

Though lions are a far greater threat to leopards of all ages than hyenas, the latter are still the bane of a leopard's life. It is often a race against time for a leopard to stash its kill in a tree before the hyenas come running, and over the years we have witnessed countless interactions between the two predators – mostly to the leopards' disadvantage. Whereas it takes up to four hyenas to force a lioness to abandon her kill, even a single hyena is usually sufficient to intimidate a leopard into relinquishing its food. For all its legendary ferocity, a leopard simply cannot afford the risk of being injured in a brawl with a hyena – particularly a female hyena, who is bigger than her male counterpart and outweighs a female leopard by 10–30kg (20–65lb).

Hyenas are incredibly powerful creatures, with bone-crushing jaws, thick muscular necks to rival a leopard's, and a matt of coarse hair that helps protect them from bites and cuts. They are quick to resort to violence if a leopard resists their attempts to steal its kill, biting the cat's rump, neck or leg to force it to drop the carcass, though if a leopard has cubs close at hand she will certainly try to defend them from attack. One female was observed to charge an overly inquisitive hyena and bite it in the rump, sending it packing – but the moment two more hyenas arrived she wisely leapt into the tree where she had stashed her kill.

I once saw Chui engage in a violent tug of war with a hyena over the remains of an impala kill that Dark had dropped out of a tree and then tried to drag away. The hyena rushed forward, ignoring Chui's hiss of warning. Dark quickly abandoned the kill and scrambled up the nearest tree. But having waited patiently until her cubs had eaten their fill, Chui was not about to surrender her meal so easily.

The situation quickly turned into the animal equivalent of a bar-room brawl. I never saw Chui quite so determined, the gathering darkness seeming to increase her aggressiveness. She charged, clawing at the hyena and sinking her dagger-like canines into his neck as he attempted to snatch the impala away. For a moment he seethed and writhed on the ground with Chui, both animals struggling ferociously for possession of the carcass. Neither dared to release their grip so as to bite the other, for fear of losing the prize altogether.

Finally, summoning all her considerable strength, Chui wrenched the kill and the hyena towards the euclea tree where the impala had originally hung. Inch by inch she forced him to follow. Eventually it was the hyena who let go, biting savagely at Chui's back leg. She did not even pause, ignoring the pain. Sensing that the battle was nearly lost, the hyena lunged forwards again, locking his powerful teeth around the impala's trailing back leg. Still Chui pulled and tugged, hauling herself closer and closer to the base of the tree. Suddenly she felt the weight release behind her as the hyena toppled backwards in an untidy heap, the impala's leg still clenched between his teeth. Chui scrambled into the tree – she was too tired to leap – leaving the hyena to race away with a portion of meat. On this occasion she had managed to turn the tables on a member of the Fig Tree Clan.

The relationship between leopards and hyenas is complex, and often has a history, with individuals of each species responding according to past experiences. Both leopards and hyenas mark out territories, so the resident leopards and the local hyena clan get to know one another and respond to one another on the basis of individual strengths and weaknesses. This is apparent in the manner in which a leopard may immediately give way to a particularly large hyena, though not all meetings are aggressive. If a leopard is resting on the ground and there is no food to contest, it often simply lies still, allowing a hyena to approach. Though hyenas have excellent vision, they rely heavily on their acute sense of smell. They tend to approach a leopard from down wind, heads bobbing as they assess the situation, making sure that there is nothing more dangerous – such as lions – in the vicinity. If the leopard has made a kill, the hyena will cock its tail and rush in with an intimidating growl to steal the food, whooping for reinforcements only if it can't manage on its own. I once saw a large female hyena charge straight at Half-Tail as she stood at the base of an acacia bush, barrelling into her with a hefty body check and putting her on the defensive, though her kill was already safely stashed 4.5m (15ft) above the ground.

Even if there is no food to contest, the hyena may still come within centimetres of the leopard's face to see if it has been eating and, if so, back-track in an attempt to pin down the location of the kill. Sometimes the leopard keeps its cool, not even bothering to growl or hiss, but if it feels threatened it twists its ears down,

revealing the black and white stripes on the backs. Mouth ajar, black lips emphasizing the long white canines, it crouches like a coiled spring. But hyenas seem singularly unimpressed by such menacing looks – they have seen it all before and know exactly how far they can go. At this point, with no food to garner, the hyena may sniff around for the leopard's droppings and eat them. Hyenas sometimes trail a leopard or a pack of wild dogs, and may even lie up close to where these predators are resting, waiting for them to set off on a hunt and then rushing in to steal the spoils.

Though female leopards rarely put up much resistance when confronted by a hyena, male leopards are larger, more aggressive and less likely to be intimidated, growling rather than hissing at hyenas and more than able to hold their own in a one-on-one encounter. The problem is that it is hard to defend a kill and eat from it at the

Chui with an impala kill stashed safely out of the reach of hyenas.

A hyena clan devouring a wildebeest. Hyenas are powerful predators, quite capable of killing adult wildebeest and zebras when hunting together. They hunt mainly at night but are also highly opportunistic and will scavenge whenever they can.

same time, and there are occasions when a leopard and a hyena may feed together on a carcass, though the minute other hyenas arrive it is time for the leopard to leave. Male leopards are more likely than females to stay in the vicinity of a kill that has been stolen from them, sometimes managing to rush in at the right moment and retrieve part of it. Otherwise the best solution is to move off quickly and hunt again.

Personality as well as size has a part to play in how predators respond to one another; degree of hunger, too, with some individuals being much more aggressive and liable to attack or to defend their property. At least two hyenas were killed by a male leopard during Bailey's study in Kruger; one was stashed in a tree, while the other was eaten on the ground. The same male was seen to attack two hyenas who tried to scavenge from a warthog he had killed, but they escaped without injury. On another occasion a large male leopard attacked and strangled a full-grown male cheetah weighing 45kg (100lb) and then

Half-Tail was completely relaxed around vehicles and quite unperturbed – it seemed – by the hustle and bustle of visitors on safari.

hoisted the carcass into a tree; a similar incident has been reported in the Serengeti.

Sometimes the tables are turned. I once saw a large male cheetah chase Beauty into a tree when she was almost fully grown. She looked most put out, snarling and grunting at the cheetah, who stared up at her and then lay down a short distance away. When Beauty climbed down from the tree the cheetah immediately charged, chasing her up a rocky hillside, where she escaped into a thicket.

It is rare to see a leopard in poor condition in the Mara, though this could be because an old or ailing leopard would soon be killed by lions or hyenas. In all the time I have spent there I have never seen a sick leopard, though I have found a number of adult cheetahs in poor condition, often due to a disease known as sarcoptic mange. Mange is caused by a tiny mite that eats away at the skin, causing the victim to scratch itself continually, tearing out the fur and opening up flesh wounds that become infected with bacteria. It is often these secondary infections that are fatal. The skin mites themselves are not usually a problem as long as the animal stays healthy. Bailey noted that mange was a significant factor in leopard mortality in the Kruger, and Lex Hess describes the Londolozi rangers being faced with the dilemma of whether or not to intervene when a leopard was suffering from mange, which is easy to treat with the right prescription.

In this instance it was a subadult who had been struggling to find sufficient food while trying to stay out of trouble with the resident adult leopards. Before the area was opened up to tourism her illness would have passed unnoticed. Is it right to offer a helping hand when your action may simply be putting other leopards under pressure? In the end the rangers decided not to interfere. The youngster then wandered onto the Mala Mala property, where she was promptly treated and recovered.

Any environmental stress such as a shortage of food during a particularly dry

winter or an increase in lion and hyena numbers may cause a rise in the animal's cortisone levels, suppressing the immune system and allowing the mites to multiply. Mange seems to be one of nature's means of controlling cat populations, and leopards at times also succumb to diseases such as anthrax, canine distemper and rabies.

There is currently a male leopard at the Nairobi Orphanage who was captured as an adult in 1985, when he was at least three years old. He must therefore be over 20 now and is somewhat arthritic; he no longer climbs into trees to rest, and has difficulty chewing his food, though he is otherwise very much alive. Half-Tail was 11or 12 years old when she died, and was fortunate to have lived as long as she did, surviving being shot in the face with an arrow by a Masai herdsman in 1997. At the time she was accompanied by a male, and one of them took a sheep or a goat, incurring the wrath of its owner. The arrow went through Half-Tail's nose and penetrated her palate, leaving a metal tip exposed and lacerating her tongue whenever she tried to close her mouth. Fortunately, drivers from Governor's Camp discovered her and one of them watched over her throughout the night, until a vet from the Kenya Wildlife Service could anaesthetize her and remove the arrow.

Though a wild leopard might be considered old by the time it is ten, in Londolozi and Mala Mala a number of animals have exceeded this lifespan – the Mother leopard lived for 14 years, and her daughter a year or so longer. But this is exceptional, particularly in areas where the slightest miscalculation in hunting large or dangerous prey – or a confrontation with a more powerful predator – could leave a leopard severely injured or dead.

Half-Tail taking a kill to safety having been disturbed by an eagle. She hid it in a croton thicket, but next morning it had gone, so she probably lost it during the night to hyenas.

The Territorial Imperative

M̲ale leopards are impressive-looking creatures, exuding a raw muscular power. I have seen so few adult males that even now whenever I happen upon one it reminds me of the old days when finding any leopard made my heart race.

During the first few years of Lex Hess's stay at Londolozi, adult male leopards seemed as shy around vehicles as those in the Mara did, and we both waited for the time when one of the male cubs that we had been able to watch would eventually settle somewhere in the area, allowing us to get a better idea of their behaviour. Today there are adult males in both our old stamping grounds who are very relaxed around vehicles, particularly in the area near Mara Intrepids Camp, which puts out bait, giving visitors the chance to watch leopards at night and helping to habituate them. The reason so many of our observations have been of females with cubs is partly that female offspring often settle as adults in an area adjacent to their mother and in some cases overlap her home range, giving birth to their cubs in favoured places that we have come to know.

Once a female leopard has established a territory she seldom strays far, living there until her death or until she is displaced by a younger rival. She demarcates the area by laying down her individual scent, reading the messages left by other passing leopards, sniffing around the bushes, fallen trees and rocks, then rubbing her face, head and body against a bush or tree before turning and spraying urine tainted with scent from her anal glands. She knows every nook and cranny of her home range, and may even choose to give birth in the same place where she herself was born. It is hardly surprising that young leopards are so reluctant to leave their natal range, or that a translocated leopard often heads straight home again after being released, regardless of the distance it must travel.

A leopard's solitary and independent nature is evident from an early age. A young lion or cheetah takes care not to

Beauty examining an interesting scent – perhaps the spot where another leopard or predator has urinated or raked its feet on the ground, leaving scent from its paws.

become separated from its companions, and if it does get left behind or lost it becomes very agitated and calls out in distress. Leopards are much more self-possessed; from the time they are barely a few months old, they grow accustomed to stopping and investigating their environment, sometimes becoming separated from their mother and siblings in the process. When this happens the leopard cub simply settles down somewhere safe – in a cave, under a bush or in a tree – and then waits for its mother to come back and find it. This independent mien increases month by month, initially driven as much by the natural way of being of a leopard as by the mother's wish to weaken the ties of kinship.

By the time a leopard is one year old it is spending the majority of its time on its own, and the changing relationship between parent and young is reinforced by the mother's increasing hostility towards her offspring. At first this is no more than a degree of impatience when the cubs try to greet her. She will bare her dagger-like canines, hiss and snarl or grunt, signalling

Half-Tail and Zawadi claw-marking the bark of an acacia tree. This helps keep their claws sharp and leaves a visible mark that other leopards can read.

that she wants to be left alone – a mixture of 'I want some peace and quiet' and 'Time to grow up and fend for yourself', in response to a cub's overt displays of affection or pestering to be fed. The bond is further weakened as a mother gradually stops leading her cub to kills, though if the young leopard is really struggling to find sufficient prey it may still be allowed to feed with her. The difference is that where before the mother would come and find her cubs, as they grow older the onus is more and more on them to find her – and kill for themselves.

A female leopard usually mates and become pregnant some months before she finally abandons her cubs. The changes that occur in the latter stages of pregnancy as she becomes even more secretive and wants to be left on her own no doubt help to put an end to contact between a mother and her previous litter, though, as we saw with Half-Tail and Beauty, there are no absolutes – a young leopard may still occasionally make contact with its mother up to the age of 20 months or more.

While watching Chui's mother, the Mara Buffalo female, with her two cubs in 1983, I was able to observe a marked difference in the development of the two sexes. I wrote at the time:

By the time the cubs were a year old the young male had abandoned Mara Buffalo Rocks as a resting place. He acted in a much more independent manner than his sister, who seemed to require a closer relationship with their mother. The male, being larger, stronger and faster, was probably better equipped to supplement the food that he still sometimes obtained from his mother's kills and he was already killing smaller game. Perhaps when only one cub is being reared, a male cub can maintain a closer association with his mother for a longer period. But in these particular circumstances there was just not enough food to go round.

On the few occasions that I was able to find the Mara Buffalo female she was still often accompanied by her daughter, at least up to the time the youngster was 14 months old. I was unable to tell what role she had played in establishing her son's more independent ways, though I noticed wounds on his back that could have been caused by a fight with another leopard.

All this is very different from the way a cheetah mother deals with her subadult offspring. There is no gradual severing of the familial bond and little sign of aggression between mother and cubs for as long as they remain together. Separation for a cheetah family normally occurs when the cubs are 14–18 months old. One day the mother simply walks away – or the cubs do. After this it is unusual for the family to make contact again, though the cubs stay together for the next few months, with female cubs then splitting off on their own and male cubs staying together for life.

Perhaps the mother's lack of aggression reflects the different land-tenure systems that cheetahs and leopards operate. Cheetah females do not defend a territory, roaming so widely – up to 800km^2 (300 sq. miles) in the Serengeti – that it would be impossible to do so. They are much more nomadic than leopards, probably due to their preference for Thomson's gazelles, which are migratory. Gaining the occasional meal from their mother once they have branched out on their own is just not an option for young cheetahs, which is perhaps why they stay with their siblings for a few months, providing them with greater vigilance against other predators and a greater chance of one of them making a kill that can then be shared.

I have never seen young cheetahs engage in real cat-fights the way leopards do over food. Sharing rather than fighting is the norm for a cheetah mother and her cubs. Time is of the essence, and there is no advantage to be gained in each waiting their turn; cheetahs cannot store kills in trees and must eat quickly and move on

The Mara Buffalo Female and her 14-month-old daughter. Daughters often end up sharing part of their mother's home range, though as adults the two leopards avoid each other.

before vultures attract hyenas or lions to the scene. Cubs occasionally compete for position by manoeuvring with their bodies or holding tight to a scrap of meat or skin and engaging in a tug of war, but a bit of low-intensity growling or churring is about as aggressive as it gets, with one or other of the cubs simply giving way or running off with a leg bone.

Lex Hess followed one young male leopard forced onto the path to independence by his mother's aggression. Rejected by her and finding it hard to obtain sufficient food for himself, he began to hang around camp and occasionally stole meat from the staff. A few weeks later he was seen trying to make contact with his mother again. She was moving, calling and scent-marking, as if she was looking for a mate. Her son was 500m (⅓ mile) away; he stopped and listened when she called and then moved towards the sound, replying with his own call and the single guttural grunt used by cubs when they are searching for their mother. Although the female chose to ignore her son's overtures, the young male picked up her scent, following in her footsteps and responding to her call whenever she gave one. At one point he was within 100m (330ft) of her, but she simply kept moving and then stopped calling. Eventually he lost her scent trail and began hanging around camp again.

Despite his tender years the young male managed to find enough food to survive

Safi greets her mother Zawadi, who responds with a discouraging snarl. This is a non-damaging way in which a mother leopard pushes her offspring towards independence.

over the next few months. At 15 months he killed a warthog piglet after a noisy confrontation with the sow. Unknown to him, his mother was only 50m (160ft) away with a kill of her own and accompanied by a new litter of cubs. Alerted by the commotion, she came to investigate, watching as the young male strangled the piglet at the base of a tree. When he looked up again he found his mother sitting

watching him. The two leopards glared at each other, the male growling quietly, the mother staring back at him. Then she crouched down facing her son, holding her ground as every so often he advanced towards her, snarling. After a few minutes she got up and moved back to where she had left her cubs. This is so cat-like, the disdain for other cats, the dislike of strangers, the sizing up of the opposition,

Subadult and young adult leopards of both sexes form a separate part of the leopard population, each with its own home range. This may initially overlap not only their mother's range but also part of their father's. Depending on the area, an adult female may be prepared to share part of her home range with her daughter as she reaches adulthood, and the daughter may be able to expand her range into that of another female (who may also be a relative). But there are bound to be times when there isn't sufficient room for this to happen, particularly if a female has already raised one or more daughters to adulthood. Under these circumstances the young female is going to have to move away, as happened with Half-Tail when she became

independent, or fight for possession with a resident, regardless of whether that is her mother, sister or an unrelated adult.

Young leopards who have dispersed (or are in the process of dispersing) from their natal range and are still searching for a place to settle have been described as 'floaters'. The males among them are usually forced to wander further afield as they mature and are hard to keep track of. If they survive – and many do not – they establish themselves in a vacant area or on the fringe of existing territories, where they may eventually be able to carve out a niche for themselves. Though the sex ratio at birth is one to one, among the adult population it is closer to one male to two females.

Zawadi looking out across her home range not far from Moses Rock, with the Siria Escarpment looming in the background. Zawadi – like Half-Tail before her – lives outside the Mara Reserve boundary, among the Masai pastoralists.

the prickly antipathy, the desire to attack and drive the intruder away tempered by the threat of those dangerous teeth and claws that can inflict such terrible injuries.

Next afternoon the young male went for a drink and then called. Hess was surprised to hear such a young leopard announcing his presence so boldly, and wondered if he was trying to locate his mother again. Having satisfied his thirst the leopard walked back up the bank, but as he crested the rise his ears went back and he bared his teeth in a snarl, flattening his body against the ground. At that moment a large male charged over the top of the bank in an intimidating display and attacked him. Both leopards tumbled down towards the water; as they reached the bottom the younger male managed to slip out from beneath his more powerful opponent and fled. The older male followed him for a while, but

Mature male lions seem less likely to attack youngsters who do not yet boast a well-developed mane. But once the nomads are four years old and begin to challenge the established order by scent-marking and roaring, there is no denying their intentions and resident pride males will defend their territory fiercely. Likewise with leopards. Older males will generally tolerate the younger generation until they are almost ready to breed, and refrain from seriously injuring a subadult, acknowledging signs of submission such as the younger male flipping onto his side and exposing his vulnerable throat.

Though serious fights are probably rare, both Patrick Hamilton and Ted Bailey found evidence of conflict when examining the leopards they had trapped and radio-collared. Some had open wounds where they had been bitten and clawed, others were scarred and showed signs of old injuries, with damage to ears, nose and eyes. Males certainly do occasionally fight tooth and nail, gladiatorial contests in which the participants rear up onto their hind legs just as male lions and tigers do, slashing and biting, breaking off and then returning to the fray until one has had enough and runs off. Injuries from a leopard's claws are more likely to cause flesh wounds; the greatest danger is of being bitten in the neck, throat or spine by those 6cm (2⅓in) canines. Dr Luke Hunter, who is currently studying leopards in Phinda Resource Reserve in South Africa, recently wrote to tell me that one of his males was killed by a four-year-old newcomer who surprised him sleeping and killed him without a struggle by a single throat bite.

A serious fight has to be over something worth fighting for, and for males that is generally control of a territory and the access to breeding females that this brings. The greatest stability comes when males have held their territories for some time, getting to know their neighbours as 'dear enemies', recognizing that they can live alongside one another if both respect the other's rights of tenure and in general keep to their own patch. But if there is any weakness or significant difference in size between males, then one may gradually take advantage of that fact – just as a larger or more experienced male lion tends to dominate a smaller or younger one in a coalition. And a female in oestrus is always likely to provoke conflict between any males in her vicinity.

Hancock and Wolhuter felt that battles for territory were often wars of attrition. They were able to follow the changing fortunes of a leopard known as the Flockfield male who settled as an adult to the south of the territories of two resident males, the Jakkalsdraai and Mlowathi males. In time the core of the Flockfield's territory shifted by over 40km (25 miles), due to pressure from his neighbours. Over a two-week period in 1994 the Flockfield and Jakkalsdraai males met regularly along their common boundary, which they marked by scuffing their hind feet, raking up the ground and claw-marking certain trees to leave a visible sign that other leopards would recognize. The two males would walk along the western bank of Boomer's Crossing, each trying to intimidate the other into backing down, parading shoulder to shoulder, salivating profusely with a mixture of pent-up aggression and fear. It was like two boxers standing eyeball to eyeball, each desperate to gain a psychological advantage. The moment one male got ahead of the other, he would attempt to move across his rival's path, prompting the other to run and try to cut him off. If either stopped they would both lower their hindquarters and scrape-mark, then roll onto their backs and rub their heads on the ground. But it never escalated beyond this show of force, as if each male was saying, 'Look how big and powerful I am, why don't you just push off before you get hurt?'

Whatever was 'said' between the two males, the message finally forced the older

next morning the youngster was back in the same area, none the worse for wear, though over the next two months he began to wander further and further afield.

In many ways young male leopards live a similar life to nomadic lions who are too young to claim a territory of their own and must roam around trying to keep out of harm's way until they are fully grown.

Flockfield male to concede the advantage and relinquish another small chunk of his territory. In other words, he was acknowledging that the Jakkalsdraai male was in the ascendancy, and would win if it came to a fight. The Flockfield male was never again seen so far north, veering off to the east for the Kruger Park whenever he reached Boomer's Crossing during his regular three-to-four-day border patrols. Eventually he spent all his time in the large plot of dense uncharted bushveld in the Kruger, and at 14 years old was still somewhere out there by the time Hancock and Wolhuter finished filming – though perhaps no longer in prime territory.

One question that is yet to be resolved is 'To what degree are female leopards territorial?' Adult females generally show little evidence of injuries from conflict with other leopards. But there is no doubt that they will chase and fight with a rival when necessary, actively defending their home range even if it isn't their exclusive preserve. As we have seen, young male leopards often mirror their mother's home range when they first become independent, and apart from competition over food pose no threat to their mother by continuing to use the area. But once young females reach breeding age, it would seem to be in their mother's interest to drive them out. However, the degree to which females adhere to this convention varies from region to region and is probably related to a number of factors – the density of the leopard population, food supply and competition with other predators.

Observers at Mala Mala and Londolozi have witnessed several encounters between mothers and daughters that provide an insight into how adult female relatives adjust to sharing parts of the same area. One incident was particularly savage and ended only when the younger female fell from a tree in which the encounter with her mother took place. Though still somewhat smaller than her mother, the daughter put up a spirited defence on being attacked.

Lex Hess describes an interaction between the Mother leopard and her subadult daughter, at a time when the Mother had two eleven-month-old cubs. She was bringing her cubs to the place where she had stashed an impala in a tree, only to find that her older daughter had discovered the kill and was already feeding. The female cub approached the tree aggressively, baring her teeth at her big sister in a throaty snarl. The older sibling snarled back; both leopards stared at each other, hissing loudly. The stand-off lasted for ten minutes, until the cub could no longer contain herself and with a loud growl rushed at her sister, springing into the tree to attack her – spurred on, no doubt, by the sense that this was her food and her territory. Finding herself on the defensive, the older sister leapt some 7m (23ft) to the ground.

The Mother leopard, who had been watching all this time, rushed forward and nipped her older daughter in the base of the tail as she turned and bounded off, ensuring that she continued on her way. The following day, the Mother was seen moving around the same area, calling and repeatedly scent-marking, probably as a result of the intrusion, though she may have been looking for a mate. The normal avoidance mechanisms had broken down and needed to be reinforced. There were no further sightings of the young female, and the Mother safely chaperoned her cubs to independence, abandoning them once they were 15 months old. Three months later she gave birth again.

In general, though, interactions between mothers and daughters are not particularly serious or damaging – a brief spat, a chase perhaps, and then it is over. In most cases females with overlapping home ranges simply avoid one another, as is illustrated by the story of another female and her daughter at Londolozi. The daughter had just failed in her attempt to ambush a herd of impala, prompting them to snort loudly in alarm. Her mother was 200m (650ft)

away at the time and, on hearing the impala, began to call, alerting her daughter to the fact that she was in the area. The young female immediately stopped and looked in the direction of the call, then walked a few metres and scraped vigorously with her hind feet before turning 90 degrees and walking away, pausing every so

Half-Tail and Zawadi. Half-Tail raised two daughters to maturity:
Beauty, who was born in 1992, and Zawadi, in 1996.

often to spray-mark bushes. The mother
then moved in the opposite direction.
Neither leopard showed any inclination to
engage in a chase, perhaps because they
were near the shared boundary of their
adjacent territories. The mother had

recently started to shift her activity further
north, allowing her daughter to establish
herself as a permanent resident in the
southern part of her former range,
something we witnessed Half-Tail do as
Zawadi matured. Having a relative as a

neighbour, someone whose habits you
know and with whom you have a shared
history, is likely to be less volatile than
accommodating an unknown leopard. In
fact relatedness may be the reason for
allowing young females to acquire a home

Zawadi suckling Safi, aged three months, on a termite mound. Leopards, like cheetahs and lions, often climb onto termite mounds for a good look round, particularly when the grass is long.

range nearby, and only by sharing at times is this possible.

The degree of tolerance shown between females is no doubt modified by the stage in their breeding cycle they are in. A mother about to give birth or with young cubs is likely to be less tolerant of intrusions, particularly when she is confined with her offspring to a relatively small part of her range, and females with young cubs are fiercely aggressive when threatened. But if a female does not constantly mark her home range it may give a younger animal or a transient adult the impression that the area is unoccupied. This might help to explain why mother leopards leave their cubs for considerable lengths of time from a young age – it is not just to hunt.

Tjellers, the female whom Hancock and Wolhuter followed, stayed very close to her den site for five days after she gave birth, then set off on a boundary patrol. She soon came across the scent of another female – the adjacent territory-holder – who had large cubs. Tjellers paused to sniff at the

ground, rolled on her back and then trotted forward, uttering a few harsh grunts and pausing briefly to listen as the intruders disappeared into the nearby lugga. There was a brief commotion as she flushed the other female from cover and chased her for 150m (500ft) before catching up with her. A brief but vicious fight took place before the females broke free and stood face to face 2m (6ft) apart, growling. Both were wounded and neither seemed keen to renew hostilities as they headed north, side by side, in the same way that male territory-holders sometimes walk parallel to one another in a boundary dispute. At one point they paused to scrape and roll on the ground, then the mother of the older cubs called to them to join her. But they were too scared to emerge from their hiding place among the bushes, and the females continued on their way, shoulder to shoulder, salivating with the stress of the encounter.

Eventually they lay down to rest 5m (16ft) apart. Ten minutes later Tjellers got to her feet and mock-charged her opponent,

who refused to give ground. After another 20 minutes, she too stood up and headed back in the direction she had come from, pausing every so often to scrape the ground with her hind feet – something that lionesses often do after an encounter with intruders or a battle with hyenas over food; it seems to boost their confidence and assert their claim to the area. Once the other female was safely on her way, Tjellers went and rolled where her adversary had marked, following her tracks for a while to confirm that she had gone.

It is evident from these illustrations that adult leopards do meet at times, and must become familiar with their neighbours, constantly assessing their strengths and weaknesses. The way a leopard behaves and how aggressively it is prepared to defend itself and its territory is modified to some degree by where the encounter takes place. The closer a leopard is to its core area – the heart of its home range – the more likely it is to fight to defend its right to that area, and the more likely a trespasser is to flee rather than stand its ground. Only when another leopard is determined to take over an area from the resident is there likely to be a serious fight.

There also seems to be a different approach to defending a home range according to whether you are male or female, as there is with lions. A male lion generally has only a short tenure as a territory-holder. His life is about maximizing breeding opportunities, and there is no time to waste. Males have been known to fight to the death in defence of their territory – or in trying to acquire one. Lionesses also defend their territory, which is passed down from one generation of females to another and is primarily a hunting ground and somewhere offering suitable hiding places for cubs – as it is for female leopards. With lions, disputes with other groups of females over territory are not quite as urgent or as viciously contested as those between rival males, though lionesses do sometimes kill a non-pride member. But generally they are long-term wars, rather than one-off battles, and this often seems to be the case with female leopards too.

One can see how the land-use system employed by solitary cats, whereby adult females tolerate their female offspring settling down in an adjacent area or even sharing part of their home range or hiving off a portion of it for themselves, allows the young females the best chance of finding living space and breeding. This could under the right circumstances evolve into an even more social way of life, with mother and daughter sharing the responsibility of raising their cubs, hunting together and defending their kills against hyenas. Which may be what gave rise to the pride system that characterizes lion society in prey-rich, savanna-type country.

The fact that many young female leopards establish themselves in or near their own natal area does pose the problem of inbreeding, with the potential for a father mating with his daughter. Hancock witnessed such an incident with one of

Tjellers' offspring. Lion society is organized in such a way that it is rare for fathers to mate with their own daughters. Lionesses don't normally breed successfully until they are in their fourth year, by which time the pride males will almost certainly have been forced out and replaced by new males to whom the females are unlikely to be related. Male leopards don't start breeding (even though they may already be sexually mature) until they have acquired a territory, by which time they are probably a minimum of three years old. In an area where competition is fierce, a territory-holder may have been displaced by the time his daughter is ready to breed, and it is also possible that most females end up settling within adjacent male territories or simply avoid mating with their father and seek out a male from an adjoining territory.

Until recently the accepted view was that apart from the few days a male and female leopard spend together when mating, they rarely meet up – in fact they avoid each other. But the years of observation at Londolozi and Mala Mala have given us a different leopard from the solitary cat described in the past. We now know that males and females living in overlapping ranges do at times meet, often without much sign of hostility, though there have been instances of males killing females. Some encounters could even be described as friendly, in as much as the leopards did not fight, nor did they seem unduly concerned by one another's presence. This is similar to reports of male and female tigers sometimes associating at a kill, or a mother socializing briefly with the father of her cubs, and they with him.

In addition to communicating by body language, cats use certain calls to reduce the possibility of aggression and signal to one another that their intentions are amicable. One such call is known as prusten or, less formally, chuffling, which I feel conveys a better sense of a sound that seems to have a touch of playfulness about it. Whatever you choose to call it, it is a

series of sharp, explosive puffing sounds like loud sniffing, made by blowing sharply through the nostrils with the mouth closed. I first heard this sound in 1983 while watching Chui summon Light and Dark from their hiding place along Fig Tree Ridge. It is a quiet and intimate call, perfect for not arousing the attention of predators; Chui often seemed to prefer to chuffle rather than use the short, sharp, rather gruff and guttural arragh-grunt that is the most commonly used contact call between a mother leopard and her cubs. The arragh-grunt is louder, and therefore more appropriate when a mother is actively searching for her cubs, unsure of their precise location; it can be modified in pitch and loudness. Though Chui often chuffled when her cubs were small, I never heard Half-Tail call in this manner, nor have I often heard Zawadi use it – both preferred the arragh-grunt.

Clouded leopards chuffle in friendly close-contact situations, as do tigers, jaguars and snow leopards. It is an integral part of the tiger's greeting behaviour, described as 'the forced exhalation of air through the nostrils and mouth, which results in a fluttering action of the lips'. Tigresses are said to chuffle most often when maintaining contact with their young, and both sexes chuffle during courtship and mating. I have never heard cheetahs or lions use this sound as a greeting, though in their book *Wild Cats of the World* Mel and Fiona Sunquist mention that 'leopards, along with lions, have a vocalization called puffing, which is analogous to the prusten of tigers, jaguars, clouded leopards, and snow leopards'. Puffing is said to be mainly articulated through the nose, though I am not convinced that, in the case of leopards at least, the sound they are making isn't chuffling or prusten. Hancock and Wolhuter heard adult leopards chuffling on a number of occasions during friendly encounters, helping to reduce tension between individuals who spend most of their time on their own.

Chui with Dark when he was three or four months old. Cubs will grizzle to be fed and, though they start eating meat from the age of seven or eight weeks, continue to suckle for the first three or four months – sometimes longer, particularly if food is scarce.

Hancock and Wolhuter once recorded the Jakkalsdraai male announcing his arrival by chuffling and being greeted in a friendly manner by Tjellers, who was accompanied by two small cubs. One might have expected her to jump up and react aggressively to the sudden arrival of a male, but the fact that she was familiar with this one and that he was probably the father of her cubs no doubt influenced her response. In fact if she had reacted aggressively she might have prompted him to attack her and her family. In any case the cubs scattered when the male let out a grunt, but he never appeared to pose a threat to them. On another occasion when the same adults sensed each other's presence they both started to chuffle – a friendly duet of reassurance analogous to 'Don't panic, everything is all right, I am not about to attack.' This is a vital form of communication between such well-armed individuals and reinforces the idea that while leopards may be primarily solitary,

they are not as antisocial as was previously thought. They learn to recognize the individual scent, call, physical bearing and temperament of other leopards in their area, and respond accordingly.

Hancock also witnessed the Jakkalsdraai male sniffing nose to nose with Tjellers after they had chuffled. The male then climbed into the tree where Tjellers had stored her kill. There was no dispute over possession of the food; the leopards simply adopted their normal feeding routine whereby one feeds alone before giving up its position to another. In this instance the cubs, who were already up in the tree, bit at their father's flank and tail as he gorged himself without provoking a violent response. This doesn't mean to say that males aren't sometimes harsh in their treatment of cubs – or so it might appear to human eyes – snarling and cuffing the youngsters when they want to be left in peace. Male lions often respond in a similarly rough fashion when young cubs

try to extend a perfunctory greeting into a play session. But even though a male might grunt out a warning, show his massive canines and bite down on the cubs to stop them bothering him, this doesn't inflict serious damage – though I have never forgotten seeing a pride male savagely attack an 18-month-old cub who was trying to hold on to a wildebeest calf that the male wanted for himself. A single bite left the cub writhing in agony, and I never saw it again. But that dispute was about food at a time when all the pride members were hungry and no quarter was given – even to their own offspring.

Like male lions, individual leopards react differently according to their age, health and temperament. The Jakkalsdraai male seemed to be particularly tolerant of Tjellers' cubs. He was seen with them on a number of occasions, and once when she had a single cub of just a few weeks old the male tracked mother and cub to their lair. Tjellers watched him approach as she lay suckling and immediately began to chuffle, prompting the male to break into a trot. The cub stopped suckling and rolled more than walked towards the male, who veered off and pushed under a bush, possibly because he was nervous that Tjellers might react aggressively towards him in the presence of such a small cub.

Lex Hess also observed a 'friendly' meeting between a male leopard and a female with two young cubs. The adults greeted, rubbing heads and intertwining their tails, then moved off together. The female was in the process of leading her cubs to a kill, and later all four leopards lay up in the tree where the carcass had been stashed, taking it in turns to feed, while a hyena waited below for any titbits. There was no sign of aggression between the leopards, underlining the theory that the reaction of one individual to another depends very much on prior experience and specific circumstances, exhibiting a degree of flexibility that makes generalizations difficult. In this instance the male remained with the female and her cubs, sharing the kill for another day, while the hyena was eventually rewarded for its persistence when the entire ribcage fell to the ground.

Some of these interactions may have been prompted by the male's desire to obtain an easy meal, which would mirror the way male lions often parasitize kills made by lionesses within their pride territory as part of the price the females pay for the males' protecting them and their cubs from the dangers posed by outsiders. The Jakkalsdraai male seemed to make a point of tracking down females in his area, checking on their sexual status and feeding on any kills they might have made – this may well be the norm for territorial males. Males sometimes even leave a partially eaten carcass to go walkabout, something a female would rarely do. Tjellers was observed taking the Jakkalsdraai male on a wild-goose chase one evening when he was trying to accompany her as she led her cubs to where she had stashed her kill. This

Chui resting at the Cub Caves with Dark and Light when they were three or four months old. By this age the cubs were old enough to be led to kills, though when Chui made a small kill she often brought it back to their hiding place for them to feed on.

prompted her to move off in the opposite direction, leading the male around her territory until he gave up. Only then did Tjellers return to finish her meal in peace.

I am convinced that there is much still to be discovered about these enigmatic cats, and that with the help of new forms of tracking devices, night-vision binoculars, image intensifiers and infrared cameras, a far more complex world will be revealed of how leopards conduct their lives.

Taratibu and Mang'aa play-fighting. At five months Mang'aa (right) was already bigger and stronger than his sister and could dominate her in this kind of situation when play became rough.

Natural-Born Killers

Male leopards are able to monitor the sexual readiness of females in their territories by analysing their scent. All cats have an organ in the roof of their mouth known as the organ of Jacobsen, which has two pit-like openings behind the front incisors. When a male comes across the scent-mark left by a female he draws back his upper lip in a grimace, sucking in a stream of air that passes over the depressions, allowing the hormone content to be analysed. If the female is coming in to season he will follow her scent trail in the hopes of mating with her.

It is a rare and exciting experience to witness leopards mating, and we were fortunate to be able to film such an event during the first series of *Big Cat Diary*: we discovered Beauty with a male on a rocky hill overlooking the upper reaches of the Bila Shaka Lugga. A leopard in oestrus is a mixture of solicitousness and aggression, and her initial response to a male may be tempered or exacerbated by previous contacts. This may lead to a degree of conflict with the female turning and rebuffing the male each time he approaches. But that generally doesn't last long. Watching Beauty consorting with her mate, we got the impression that she was the one taking the initiative. It was almost comical at times to see the seductive manner in which she approached the male, moving rapidly towards him from her

resting place in the grass a few metres away. She paced around him, changing position so quickly that at first he looked somewhat bemused. I described the occasion in *Mara–Serengeti: A Photographer's Paradise:*

When we first discovered the mating couple they were secluded in a patch of thick croton bush on top of a rocky hill bordering the northern end of the Bila Shaka Lugga. The male was huge – he looked almost twice the size of Beauty – with a dark coat and floppy tip to his spotted tail. Beauty was in

the height of oestrus, and so hyped up that she could hardly keep still for more than a minute or so at a time. She slunk towards the male, whipping round and shoving her hindquarters provocatively in his face before sitting on his head for good measure, pushing up under his chin and nudging him into a sitting position. Then she darted forward and crouched, ears laid back, growling. No sooner had the male mounted her than he reached sharply forward and gaped across her neck,

Half-Tail making a flehmen face. This is the way all cats analyse scent, drawing an odour into their mouths and testing it.

Zawadi yawning. A leopard's long canines are used to grasp and kill its prey.

Beauty, aged six months, resting in a tree along the Ngorbop Lugga. She settled to the east of her natal home range, but continued to share part of the area with her mother.

Mating leopards show little interest in food, though like lions they will take advantage of any prey that wanders within range. On the one occasion that mating leopards were seen to make a kill, they abandoned their food before it was finished and resumed their meanderings. Other people who have observed leopards mating have commented on how the male often leaps to one side after ejaculating, sometimes vaulting right over the female's head in an attempt to avoid her turning and slapping him. Lionesses sometimes act in a similarly aggressive manner after mating, perhaps because a cat's penis has tiny, backward-pointing spines that are thought to help stimulate ovulation in some way, perhaps by roughening the wall of the vagina.

That was the first time I had seen Beauty for more than two and a half years. By then she was four years old, so there was a chance that she had already had one litter and was ready to mate again. But nobody had reported seeing her with cubs, so it was possible that she had yet to raise any. Once she became independent Beauty was never the same carefree, trusting leopard that she had been in the company of her mother. She came to resent the intrusion of vehicles into her life. It was all too apparent that she

exposing his long dagger-like canines. As Beauty rumbled – a low, deep growl – he let out a high-pitched gurgling noise, a most unexpected and extraordinary throaty explosion of stuttering, quite unlike the sound made by a mating lion.

A pattern quickly became apparent. Every 50 minutes or so, Beauty would initiate another bout of mating, the act itself lasting no more than ten seconds, with intervals of only a few minutes before another coupling,

repeated four or five times in all – then silence as both cats lay flat in the long grass, hidden from view. One evening a few weeks later we found the pair mating again. Beauty must have failed to conceive and come back into oestrus. They had been seen together in Leopard Gorge and by the time we arrived had moved to a hillside covered with long grass. The area was a minefield of concealed rocks, but we were able to inch forward; at one point Beauty came wanted to be left alone and would charge any car that came too close – and many did. Beauty chose to retreat into that secret world that many leopards inhabit, unseen by humans for much of their lives. Some time later I was told that she had been seen with cubs, though I have never again been able to track her down myself. If she is still alive she would be ten years old – old by leopard standards.

Dale Hancock and Kim Wolhuter were able to observe an interesting sequence of events when Tjellers came into season some ten months after giving birth to her previous litter and mated with the Jakkalsdraai male. When the courting couple came across Tjellers' cubs, the two youngsters fled at the sounds of mating. Tjellers failed to conceive, perhaps because she was not yet ready to become a mother again or because the chances of a female conceiving are fairly poor – Bailey gives a figure of just 15 per cent for the likelihood that a female will become pregnant from any one mating session, mirroring the low conception rate – 20 per cent – reported for lions.

A month later Tjellers mated again with the same male, and again failed to conceive. These monthly mating sessions continued over the next few months and lasted for up to six days, until finally a second male was heard calling to the north-west. Tjellers almost immediately set off in his direction. The Jakkalsdraai male tried to head her off, prompting her to crouch down and hiss at him defensively. Little by little she managed to move towards the other male, with the Jakkalsdraai following her, until eventually she crossed out of her home range. They were now on the boundary of the Jakkalsdraai's territory and suddenly found themselves face to face with the Mlowathi male. Tjellers immediately acted submissively, though it didn't prevent the male from attacking her.

The Mlowathi male then chased the Jakkalsdraai back to his territory, both of them calling repeatedly. Tjellers followed

the Mlowathi male into his territory, though by now she was far from home. For as long as she remained with the male she would be safe from attack, but once she had finished mating she would have to negotiate a way home alone, hoping to avoid contact with any resident females in the area. This mating too proved unsuccessful, and a month later she mated with the Jakkalsdraai male again and produced a single cub. All this had taken nearly a year, by which time the cubs from her previous litter were 21 months old and capable of looking after themselves.

Research in India provides insights into the life of another solitary big cat, the tiger, indicating that fights between males are most likely to occur when a female is in oestrus and males transgress the normal limits of their territories in an attempt to mate. Male tigers have much shorter reproductive lives than females, anything from seven months to six years with an average of just under three years, half that of females. Male tigers who lost their territories within their first year of residency did not manage to sire any offspring – none that survived, at least.

In another study two female tigers bred successfully for many years until they were eventually ousted from their territories, and though they survived to the ages of 13½ and 15½ years respectively, neither managed to breed again having lost the security of a home range. It is evident that, as with leopards, a stable system of land tenure yields greater breeding success for territory-holders. Up to 90 per cent of tiger cubs in this study survived when there were no takeovers, but when resident males died or lost their territories, widespread infanticide reduced cub survival to 30 per cent. In Bandhavgarh, where the male tiger population is less numerous than in most other reserves, challenges are infrequent, and a male called Charger held a territory for ten years and lived to the age of 17 – far older than might otherwise have been expected.

When people first began to report incidents of infanticide among lions it was thought to be an aberrant form of behaviour. But it has since been reported in tigers and leopards, and can be viewed as normal – imperative even. Infanticide by a new male territory-holder helps to ensure that he has the best chance not only of siring cubs, but of remaining in the area long enough to provide a stable environment in which they can grow up: it takes a minimum of two years from conception for tigers and leopards to become independent. Infanticide simply speeds up the process of change, wiping the genetic slate clean by obliterating the offspring of the previous territory-holder, and in the process reducing competition for food from the offspring of other males.

Infanticide is found mainly among rodents and carnivores, but is also relatively common in many primate societies. Indian langurs and gorillas lose up to 30 per cent of their young to males impatient to breed, and losses of as high as 60 per cent have been reported in red howler monkeys in South America. The prevalence of infanticide seems to be exacerbated by the

Half-Tail coaxing Beauty from under a safari vehicle. Big cats in the Mara become so used to vehicles that they virtually ignore them.

*L*ions, being social, adopt a different strategy to rearing cubs from that employed by leopards and tigers. Male lions spend a considerable amount of time in the company of the lionesses in their pride (though this may vary from area to area), gaining food from any kills the lionesses make, and often remaining close to lionesses with cubs – their cubs – particularly when these are small and at their most vulnerable. This helps ensure that strange males do not have the opportunity to kill them. Leopards do not live like this. Instead of investing time and energy in staying close to a female and her cubs and possibly compromising her ability to hunt successfully, a male leopard spends most of his time – when not sleeping or resting – patrolling his territory, laying down a web of scent-marks and scrapes along its boundaries, as well as calling and at times making himself conspicuous to let any potential rivals know that the area is already under management. This means covering his territory on a regular basis, sometimes travelling 10 km (6 miles) or more in a night in an attempt to deter any rival from settling in the area. Even so, infanticide is a real threat for small cubs. Any time a territorial male dies or is displaced, the new territory-holder will certainly try to hunt down and kill any cubs too young to escape.

The elder of the Topi Plains males mating with Mama Lugga, one of the Marsh Lionesses, after taking over her pride.

long period of dependency of the young of these species and their need to remain constantly with their mothers, making it relatively easy for males to identify which females are not currently receptive to breeding. Under these circumstances it would make sense for a male to stay with any female with whom he has consorted to

The Topi Plains male guards Mama Lugga to prevent any rivals from approaching and mating with her.

protect his offspring against infanticide by new males – and to help deter any other predator from attacking his young. The fearsome canines of many monkeys probably evolved as weapons to intimidate rivals in the race to breed, with the added benefit of being highly effective as a defence against predators.

Whenever a male lion finds a female in season he immediately begins to follow her, staying within a metre or so to prevent any other male from gaining access to her. His coalition partners must wait their turn – sometimes after two or three days the first male loses interest in the female, enabling one of the others to mate with her. This seemingly promiscuous behaviour on the part of the female may be essential to the well-being of any cubs born to the pride after a takeover. If the males have mated with a number of different lionesses in the

pride and sometimes with the same female(s) as their coalition partners, none of them can be sure who has fathered any cubs that are born. This helps ensure that the males provide equal support in defending the cubs and do not try to kill them – they all act in a paternal way. In all probability every male lion who manages to take over a pride has been a cub-killer at some point in his life, and probably so have most male leopards – they have no option if they are to fulfil their sexual imperative and sire as many cubs as possible during their tenure as territory-holders.

I had seen male lions indulge in infanticide, but never thought I would encounter it with leopards. Then one morning towards the end of 1997 Angie and I witnessed just such an incident in Leopard Gorge. We were working on an American television series called *Wild*

Cubs from the Marsh pride trying to suckle from their mother on a termite mound.

Things, which was very much a forerunner of the 'actuality' style that *Big Cat Diary* was developing, relying on presenters to bring to life the excitement and wonder of spending time with wild animals in exotic locations. In July, when Zawadi was a year and a half old, Half-Tail had mated again, and in early October had given birth to her fifth litter. By this stage there was little or no contact between the two leopards, though their home ranges overlapped considerably. When Angie and I heard that Half-Tail had cubs we decided to head to the Mara with a *Wild Things* film crew.

On arrival we tracked down our friend Enoch Isanya, one of the driver-guides at Mara River Camp. Over the past few years Enoch had spent months at a time following Half-Tail and her various litters as a guide to Fritz Polking, who had recently written a book on the Mara's most famous leopard. The previous evening Enoch had seen Half-Tail carrying a tiny cub from one cave to another and felt certain that there was another cub in there as well. We were excited at the prospect of some excellent filming opportunities with both Half-Tail and Zawadi, who had been seen around Observation Hill 1km (⅔ mile) to the east of Leopard Gorge.

A ten-week-old cub playing with its mother's tail. Cubs love to play with their mother's tail – indeed, any twitching tail tip is irresistible.

The following morning we found Half-Tail in the gorge, relaxed as ever, pausing to spray her scent against the bumper of one of the vehicles, then using another as cover to scrutinize a herd of impalas. She moved carefully, checking for hares among the tangles of grass at the base of acacia trees that had been felled by passing elephants, sniffing and spraying bushes and boulders, leaving a scent trail that would tell other leopards she was in residence and that they should avoid the area.

That evening we were told that Half-Tail had killed a Thomson's gazelle on Observation Hill and had stashed it in a tree. But when we arrived at the spot the following morning we found Zawadi feasting on the kill. Perhaps the driver had been mistaken and it had been the younger female all the time, or perhaps Zawadi had found her mother's kill and taken possession of it while she was preoccupied with suckling her new cubs back at the gorge. Leopards are not averse to scavenging, and as we have seen male leopards sometimes feed from a kill made by a female in his territory. But generally adult females give each other a wide berth, and stay close to a kill until it is finished.

The following morning we drove back to Leopard Gorge in the hope of finding Half-Tail, but none of us was prepared for what happened next. Our support vehicle had spotted a leopard in the gorge and called us on the radio. When we arrived we saw immediately that it wasn't Half-Tail. This leopard was shy and had a tail. In fact it was a young male with a pink nose and unmarked ears – he was in perfect condition. At first I thought it might be Mang'aa, Half-Tail's son, who was almost four years old by now and still occasionally seen in the area, though mostly further to the west. But this leopard was not as dark as Mang'aa, nor as relaxed around vehicles. He had a pale-coloured coat and certainly wasn't the male we had seen mating with Beauty the previous year, who we imagined had also fathered Half-Tail's latest litter.

Angie and I felt distinctly uneasy. The male looked nervous and was obviously in the process of investigating the area, almost certainly searching for where Half-Tail had hidden her cubs. Though the scent trail that Half-Tail had lain down around the gorge would serve to deter other adult females from using the area, her only defence against other males was the presence of a territorial male. Was this young male the new territory-holder? Had he managed to chase the older incumbent away, and was he now searching for mating opportunities of his own? Perhaps the territory-holder had been killed or died, opening the door to newcomers. To add to the mystery,

A young male leopard prowling around the entrance to Leopard Gorge, searching for Half-Tail's latest litter.

another vehicle found two dead bush hyrax, their fur partially plucked, lying on a rock at the base of the gorge near where Half-Tail's cubs were hidden. Had she sensed the presence of the male earlier in the morning and quickly moved away, abandoning her meal?

Every so often the young male paused to sniff the rocks, silently continuing his search, wary perhaps of a surprise encounter with the old female. Suddenly he dropped down behind one of the boulders and disappeared into a clump of long grass shielding the mouth of a cave. Moments later he reappeared with a tiny cub in his mouth, clasping it around the waist like a cat with a mouse. There was blood on the neck of the lifeless body. He dropped the cub behind the rock face, then entered the cave again and re-emerged with a second cub. Later he checked the cave for a third time, but there were no more cubs for him to kill. We imagined he ate the little corpses before continuing along the top of the gorge.

We spotted Half-Tail resting in a tree about 200m (⅛ mile) away. Had she seen the male prowling around the top of the gorge?

She certainly must have seen the two young lions that appeared on the scene an hour or so later. The male leopard did and, after watching them approach for a while, wisely slunk away.

Later, Half-Tail returned to the gorge. She could obviously smell the male long before she reached the place where she had left her cubs. At one point she leapt aside

as she crept around the rocks, appearing fearful. She did not enter the cave but, having carefully sniffed around the vicinity, continued towards a giant fig tree that stands like a sentinel above the west rim of the gorge. What she didn't realize was that the male leopard had seen her coming and was crouching among the rocks. A violent confrontation must then have taken place, because the next thing we saw was Half-Tail bounding up the trunk of the fig tree, taking refuge among the topmost branches. The male chased after her, and before I had time to move the vehicle one of the leopards toppled backwards out of the tree in a shower of leaves and twigs – a fall of more than 6m (20ft). Surely it must have been Half-Tail. But no – it was Half-Tail who climbed down the broad trunk of the fig tree, hissing out a warning to the male to move on. We gave a silent cheer for the gutsy female as the young male skulked off, followed at a distance by Half-Tail, limping on a bloodied forepaw.

Half-Tail resting in a tree within view of Leopard Gorge, a few hundred metres from where the male was killing her cubs. It is hard for a female to challenge a male – they are so much bigger and stronger.

The young male emerges with one of the cubs which he had already bitten in the neck and killed. Both cubs were killed in this fashion and probably eaten.

We stayed with Half-Tail for most of the rest of the day. She lay among the blackened stubble on the flank of the gorge, spittle drooling from her lips. She seemed anxious and distressed, but made no attempt to return to the place where she had last left her cubs, as if she knew that they had gone.

The father of Half-Tail's cubs would certainly have vigorously contested the presence of this young adult male, fighting if necessary to drive him away. But a male's territory is large, and he can't be everywhere at once. Other males are bound to slip through at times, and young ones wander widely when searching for a place to settle. Sooner or later, every territory-holder must face the challenge posed by younger, fitter males. Killing cubs is a natural part of the cycle by which males win and lose the rights to a breeding territory. If ever a creature was designed to sniff out the place where a mother leopard has hidden her cubs, it is another leopard.

A few weeks later a friend reported seeing Half-Tail mating with a large male in a patch of forest just above the spring that feeds Musiara Marsh. At one point she followed him across the Mara River, but returned a day or so later. By the time we began filming the second series of *Big Cat Diary* in early September 1998, she had given birth to her sixth litter and had moved further north, forced perhaps to relinquish Leopard Gorge and Fig Tree Ridge to Zawadi.

If the young male who had killed Half-Tail's previous litter did succeed in establishing himself in the area, he certainly wasn't the only one to have access to Fig Tree Ridge and Leopard Gorge: during the filming of our third series in 2000 we were fortunate to be able to catch glimpses of another adult male, and this one was unmistakable. Droopy Jaw, as he became known, was distinguished by an old injury or deformity to his lower jaw that had left the front half (between his back teeth and

Wildbeest streaming over the ridge leading to Musiara Marsh. They can always find water here during the dry season, though the Marsh Lions regularly lie in wait for them among the reedbeds.

his canines) drooping whenever his mouth was ajar. I doubt if he would have lived had he been born with such a pronounced deformity, so perhaps a zebra foal had lashed out and kicked him as he attempted to pull it down, and he had somehow survived while it healed. One thing was not in dispute – he was in perfect health now, proving just how resourceful and tough leopards are: the injury didn't prevent him from killing or eating.

On one occasion we filmed Droopy Jaw ambushing a wildebeest calf in Leopard Gorge. He was a wily character, waiting until he spotted a calf and then rushing to intercept the herd as it picked its way down a narrow pathway, knowing exactly the right moment to launch his charge up the slope. It was noticeable studying the videotape later that he had to maintain his grip on the calf's throat for longer than one might otherwise have expected, presumably because he couldn't bring his lower canines into play to apply the normal vice-like stranglehold to its full extent. He was seen successfully adopting the same strategy on a number of occasions to kill wildebeest calves, though the hyenas sometimes managed to steal his partially eaten meals before he could drag the remains into a tree.

If in fact Droopy Jaw was the new territory-holder, Zawadi was highly suspicious of his intentions. We saw her engaging him in a violent cat-fight one morning when he surprised her with Safi, who was then a year old: he suddenly dropped from his hiding place in the dense crown of a tree on Moses Rock and confronted mother and daughter. This made me suspect that Safi was not his cub – or perhaps he was checking if Zawadi was ready to mate. But Zawadi was taking no chances and briefly fought with Droopy Jaw, then moved parallel to him, blocking his path to give Safi time to escape. Neither adult seemed to want to risk unnecessary injury, and after two such scraps involving lots of grunting and snarling, Zawadi forced the male to move on. She then back-

Zawadi resting on a termite mound near Moses Rock. She still returns to Leopard Gorge and Fig Tree Ridge, where she was born, to have her own cubs.

tracked to the place where Safi had disappeared, and spent the rest of the day in a state of some anxiety. We waited with her. As the sky darkened she called repeatedly – not the loud, long-distance contact call, but the guttural 'arragh-grunt'. Eventually, having hidden herself away in a thicket, Safi reappeared and joined her mother.

A few days later we filmed Zawadi calling, perched conspicuously on top of a termite mound, and wondered if she was looking for her daughter or trying to locate a mate. I was mesmerized to see Zawadi making her contact call at such close range – she was only metres from our vehicle. Just as a lion puts maximum effort into roaring, so too does a leopard, lowering its head and stretching out its neck, forcing the air bellows-like from its lungs, sides heaving with the effort. Each time Zawadi finished a series of eight or ten calls, she listened intently. She obviously expected or hoped for an answer, or for Safi to find her. It was around this time that we saw Safi scent-mark for the first time, so perhaps this was an indication that she intended to try to stay on in the area.

There was no sign of Droopy Jaw while we were working on series four, though that didn't mean that he wasn't still in the area. But during the last few weeks of filming we managed to track down another adult male. One of our game-spotters had caught sight of a large male leopard hiding in a patch of forest to the east of Leopard Gorge. A week earlier we had finally caught up with Safi again in this same area. She was now three years old and ready to become a mother herself, but she had never been as comfortable with vehicles as Zawadi and was only occasionally seen.

When I arrived at the place where the male was hidden, I could just make out part of his long spotted tail and a patch of coat among the dense foliage of a tree. In situations like this you are left wondering how on earth anyone ever finds a leopard, and thinking of the countless times you

Zawadi and Safi resting on a termite mound. At the time of writing, Safi is in her fourth year. She shares part of her mother's home range and should soon give birth to her first litter of cubs.

must have driven past one, searching, searching, yet finding nothing to suggest that the leopard was there all the time, watching you from its hiding place as you continued on your way.

Moments later the leopard suddenly peered out at us from the canopy before hurrying down the tree and disappearing from view. That was the last we would see of him, I thought – but then a mother warthog emerged from her burrow at the edge of the lugga and trotted straight towards where the leopard must have been watching. The male couldn't resist the chance of a kill and reappeared, even though he looked as if he had already eaten a huge meal. But the warthog was having none of it – turning at the last minute and confronting the male, she stopped him in his tracks and forced him to abandon the hunt. This time I got a good look at him through my binoculars. The minute I had him in my sights I knew that it was the male that Angie and I had watched kill Half-Tail's cubs in Leopard Gorge, almost exactly five years earlier. He had that same russet-ginger coat and dog-like face. More importantly, when I leafed through the identification album that our son David had compiled for us, there he was – the same spot pattern – everything matched.

It was ironic to think that this was probably the male who had recently been seen mating with Safi, Half-Tail's grand-daughter. Had he been displaced by Droopy Jaw or did the two males' territories overlap? With males being so difficult to observe I couldn't be sure if just one male patrolled Half-Tail's old home range and also included the overlapping home ranges of her daughters Beauty and Zawadi within his territory, an area of more than 60 km² (22 sq. miles). It was certainly possible. That is the fascination in trying to follow the lives of these beautiful, enigmatic creatures. There are always new questions to try to answer.

Zawadi searching for prey from the top of an acacia tree. It is amazing how leopards are able to clamber around in these trees without constantly getting thorns in their feet.

The World of Cats

The leopard is a solitary and secretive inhabitant of thickets, an animal of darkness. These characteristics have been both its salvation and its doom. By remaining out of sight, it has been able to survive near dense human habitation, areas from which other large cats have long vanished. But, whereas the lion invokes good will by displaying its indolent, seemingly carefree nature, the leopard conveys visions of a nocturnal marauder, of a cold, detached personality. Friendliness leads to friendliness. By virtue of its being so withdrawn the leopard has received little sympathy from man and now desperately needs it. Persecuted for its lovely hide, it maintains only a precarious foothold where it was formerly abundant. Every woman who needs to satisfy her vanity with a leopard-skin coat should first contemplate the exquisite beauty of this cat in repose.

George Schaller
Serengeti: Kingdom of Predators

The lion, tiger, and leopard are no longer simply emblems on flags and signet rings. They are flesh-and-blood creatures with a past and a present, as are the secretive mountain lion and jaguar of the Americas. Myths have been replaced with fact. We know what diseases lions and leopards suffer from, what parasites infect them, and we can supplement the findings of field studies with a wealth of information gleaned from research on cats in zoos and safari parks. There is even a Cat Specialist Group, part of the Species Survival Commission (SSC) of the World Conservation Union (IUCN), which helps to monitor the status of cats worldwide and publishes a twice-yearly newsletter, *Cat News*.

Radio-telemetry and its even more modern cousins the satellite collar and computer-chip implants mean that cats, and many other animals from polar bears to humpback whales, can now be tracked as they journey over vast areas – 1000km (625 miles) or more in the case of whales. Elsewhere camera traps, triggered automatically by the subject treading on a pressure pad or breaking an infrared beam, have proved highly successful in establishing the numbers of tigers and jaguars in forest reserves where it is difficult to radio-track individuals. Such traps would be a relatively cost-effective way of obtaining data on leopard densities in Africa's tropical rainforests, where little is known about their numbers.

Trying to come up with realistic figures for the world's total leopard population has proved difficult. Nobody knows how many leopards exist in most areas where they are protected, let alone on private land or country by country. Ironically the leopard is abundant enough to be considered a pest in some parts of its range, although it is critically endangered in others. This has prompted heated debate between those who favour seeing it utilized, either as a hunting trophy or for trade in its spotted coat, and those who remind us that before these activities were banned they had a serious impact on many leopard populations. When I arrived in Africa in 1974 all leopards were listed as vulnerable

Safi and her brother at three months old. Leopard cubs are very playful, amusing themselves for hours while their mother is away hunting or patrolling her range.

Translocating giraffes from a game ranch in Namibia to a sanctuary in South Africa. Southern African countries apply a 'use it or lose it' policy to game management on private land, and game-ranching and trophy-hunting are lucrative industries

by the IUCN and continued to be so until I published my first book, *The Marsh Lions*, in 1982, by which time a new generation of leopards was just beginning to show itself. During this period all international trade in leopards was banned. There is no question that the depredations of the skin trade put the worldwide leopard population at risk – in 1969 it was estimated that 50,000 leopards were killed every year in Africa alone to supply the fur trade.

Since 1983, the Central African Republic, Ethiopia, Kenya (where hunting has been banned since 1977), Tanzania, Malawi, Zambia, Zimbabwe, Botswana, Mozambique, Namibia and South Africa have all been entitled to provide export quotas for leopards hunted as trophies, and as such the trophies may be imported into the United States. However, leopards are still classified by the United States as endangered throughout the rest of their historic range – the remainder of Africa, Asia Minor, India, South-East Asia, China, Malaya and Indonesia – and commercial trade in all leopard products is banned under Appendix 1 of the Convention on the International Trade in Endangered Species

(CITES). (Appendix 1 lists animals 'that are threatened with extinction and that are or may be affected by international commercial trade'.) Thankfully the trade in leopard skins experienced a remarkable decline in the 1970s, prompted in part by a highly effective advertising campaign that helped to make wearing a leopard-skin coat in public an anathema. But recently there has been a worrying trend among the young rich to sanction the wearing of a fur coat as chic, and certain countries such as Germany, Japan and parts of South America have never lost their appetite for this particular 'fashion'. The memorable '70s catchphrase 'It takes the skins of 20 dumb animals to make a fur coat, but only one dumb bitch to wear it' remains etched in my consciousness.

There are people who argue that hunting and trade are justifiable on the basis that they can serve conservation efforts by generating revenue from wildlife. Tanzania, for example, currently earns more foreign exchange from trophy-hunting than from wildlife-based tourism. And in many parts of Africa the sale of skins of leopards who had killed livestock and were then shot,

provided a degree of compensation for the livestock owners. Loss of this form of recompense prompted some ranchers to try to eradicate all predators. But the re-opening of trade is always likely to pose serious problems for the authorities. This has certainly proved the case with ivory. How do you control consumptive utilization so that the age-old abuses of the system don't come back to haunt you, particularly in countries in East and southern Africa where a well-developed tourist industry thrives on the ability to show visitors big cats? Wildlife-based tourism is still the mainstay of Kenya's conservation ethos, while most southern African countries prefer to follow the 'use it or lose it' philosophy, where game-ranching and trophy-hunting compete with wildlife tourism for the tourist dollar.

A compromise is probably the only way forward, and the hunting of leopards as trophies – distasteful as it may be – may continue to be viewed as sound management practice, provided proper quotas are established and honoured. But opening up the trade in skins would seem to be asking for trouble.

In the 1970s South Africa was believed to have the greatest number of fur dealers in Africa and acted as a convenient conduit to world markets for skins from elsewhere on the continent. Many of the skins were obtained illegally, with prices averaging $250–300 between 1966 and 1972, with a high of $680. In his book *The African Leopard*, Ted Bailey maintains that 'any relaxation of existing regulations or amendments that might create loopholes in those regulations should be considered with extreme caution; such loopholes in those regulations might once again trigger a dramatic increase in the numbers of leopards illegally killed for their skins.'

Supporters of consumptive utilization on a sustainable basis might disagree. Dr Anthony Hall-Martin, Director: Research and Development of the National Parks Board of South Africa, says, 'The only really honest argument against the harvesting of African leopard skins is the possibility that an open market may conceivably represent a threat to leopards in Asia – where they are threatened.' Hall-Martin feels that under the right circumstances, and if rigorously controlled, trophy-hunting should still be permitted. Referring to southern African countries he says, 'In these arid southern savannas, the hunting industry has evolved into a paying partner of the cattle industry. One of the prizes remains the leopard, Africa's ultimate spotted cat, and a trophy leopard will add up to US$4,000 on top of daily rates. This ends up giving the leopard a significant cash value. There is considerable incentive, therefore, to maintain breeding populations of leopards to service the hunting industry. The extermination of leopards as a result of trophy-hunting is most unlikely.'

If this attitude is going to prevail, quotas based on scientific studies will be needed to ensure that areas are not overhunted, and both quotas and ethical hunting practices will have to be rigorously enforced. For example, taking too many adult male leopards year after year from the same area may encourage a continual influx of new males, making it difficult for resident females to breed successfully. Loss of established territory-holders opens the door to newcomers eager to begin breeding – and they are liable to kill any young cubs.

Another worry arises from the barbaric practices that have crept into the hunting industry in recent times. A business known as canned hunting has sprung up in certain southern African countries, notably South Africa, where in particular lions – not wild lions, but lions bred in captivity – are released into large enclosures for trophy-hunting purposes. In one well-publicized incident the lion was drugged beforehand to make the job of killing it as easy as possible for the client. To preserve the 'trophy', the lion sometimes endures an agonizing death, shot in the back or abdomen to ensure that the head and

mane are undamaged, rather than being dispatched with a brain shot. To add to this, leopards are sometimes hunted with dogs, chased until they take refuge in a tree and then shot either with a rifle or with bows and arrows. The popularity of this kind of leopard-hunting has perhaps been increased by the ban on hunting mountain lions with dogs in the United States. Fortunately, an international outcry prompted by an exposé on television and in the print media is leading to these kinds of practices being banned in South Africa.

The expansion of the human population and its livestock over vast parts of Africa's woodlands and savannas is the greatest threat to both leopards and lions, particularly due to the loss of their natural prey. Ranchers often eliminate wild game in an attempt to reduce competition for valuable grazing and browse, leaving large predators little choice but to kill stock. The fact that leopards are creatures of habit, frequenting well-used paths and scent-posts, makes individuals easier to eradicate than might be thought. Even a creature as

adept at living close to humans as the leopard has little chance of survival once it incurs man's wrath and is faced with a lethal combination of traps, poison (organochlorine pesticides are a cheap and easily available poison) and guns.

Though we can be certain that there are many more leopards in Africa than the combined total for lions (maximum of 30,000, possibly as few as 20,000) and cheetahs (12–15,000) – and that as a species it is not currently in danger of extinction – various attempts to estimate how many leopards survive in the wild have failed to establish an accurate figure. Under intense lobbying from the powerful trophy-hunting industry, which was anxious to see the leopard downlisted as an endangered species, in 1987 CITES commissioned two scientists to provide population estimates for the 38 African countries where leopards were still known to exist. By then I had written *The Leopard's Tale* and was working in the Serengeti on a book on wild dogs. I met the two scientists concerned – Rowan Martin of the Zimbabwe Department of

Elephants enjoying a mud wallow at the spring feeding Musiara Marsh.
Mud helps elephants to keep cool and is a perfect skin conditioner.

National Parks and Wildlife Management and Tom de Meulenaer, a Belgian biologist – somewhere out in the vastness of the short-grass plains. They had developed a computer model to help them answer the question that everyone was asking. By feeding in information on rainfall and habitat country by country, they felt it should be possible to calculate the abundance of suitable prey, and from that extrapolate the number of leopards each area could sustain. By this process they estimated the leopard population for sub-Saharan Africa to be 714,105. But when they presented their findings to the Secretariat of CITES, who in turn asked for comments from experts, it caused a furore. One of the biggest weaknesses of the study was that it had been apparent for some time that certain areas which had previously supported healthy leopard populations no longer did so, and Martin and de Meulenaer's calculations did not take this into account. If the figure of 700,000 were true, it would have been sufficient to warrant moving the leopard from the endangered list to threatened, prompting the easing of protective measures such as the international ban on trade in leopard skins.

Fortunately, the general consensus among field biologists who had studied leopards in Africa was that there might be less than half the number that Martin and de Meulenaer suggested – 350,000 leopards – leading CITES to reject any change in protective measures for the species. Interestingly, Viv Wilson, who studied duikers in the Central African Republic, which has always been thought to represent good leopard habitat, maintained that in this particular instance 'there was no relationship whatsoever between leopard densities, habitat and rainfall. The rainfall in the area is at least 1,524mm (60in) a year; there are hundreds of square kilometres of ideal leopard habitat, large numbers of blue duiker; and yet leopard numbers are very low.' The reason for the paucity of leopards was that they had been virtually exterminated many years earlier and were only just beginning to recover.

In South Africa, where Martin and de Meulenaer gave an estimate of 23,472

Half-Tail resting in a giant fig tree along Fig Tree Ridge. A leopard without cubs spends much of the day resting and sleeping, waiting until it is cool before setting off to hunt or patrol its home range.

leopards, one reviewer suggested that fewer than 3,000 leopards survived, and Ted Bailey felt that even this figure could be too high, taking into account that his estimate for the vast protected area of the Kruger National Park was only about 700.

There is no doubt that there are still many leopards in Africa: in some areas they are extremely common. But equally there is no question that their range is shrinking worldwide, with the vast majority occurring in sub-Saharan Africa. The fact that so many subspecies have been described over the years attests both to how wide-ranging the leopard is and to how fragmented and isolated some of the populations have become. They are still found scattered across North Africa, Arabia and through Central Asia to the Far East. But while African and South Asian leopards are numerous, the other subspecies occur in small or geographically isolated populations, most of which are at risk.

Little is known about the status of the leopard in much of Asia. We do know that by the mid-1970s it was still abundant in the larger forests of India and Nepal and in the Alborz Mountains of Iran, and that it was present in the Karchat Hills of Pakistan. Its numbers have been greatly reduced throughout China, and in Sri Lanka they are on the decline outside parks and reserves. The Barbary leopard of North Africa clings on in the Central Atlas Mountains and forests of Oulmes in Morocco, but is separated from other leopard populations by hundreds or perhaps thousands of kilometres, and the Zanzibar leopard *Panthera pardus adersi* is almost certainly extinct. The Anatolian leopard is on the brink, with only a few scattered individuals recorded in south-western Turkey, and leopards in the deserts of southern Israel are faring little better. The most northern subspecies, the Amur or Far Eastern leopard (also known as the Korean leopard), *P. p. japonensis*, is now largely confined to several reserves in North Korea and the Maritime Territory of Russia

Chui with a young impala at dawn, waiting for hyenas to retire to a shady spot, so she can carry her kill back to her cubs.

and numbers fewer than 100 individuals. That means that there are fewer Amur leopards in the wild than in the world's zoos. The largest single population numbers about 30 and a recovery plan awaits the support of federal and regional governments in China and Russia.

The struggle of isolated leopard populations to survive is illustrated by recent attempts to protect what is probably physically the smallest of all leopard subspecies, *Panthera pardus nimr*, the Arabian leopard – or nimr, as it is known locally. The Arabian leopard once occurred throughout the mountains of southern Arabia, where its small size and pale coat with small, widely spaced spots are adaptations to the bare, rocky areas in which it lives. It is now highly endangered due to hunting and loss of habitat to livestock, and by 1990 had become locally extinct in most areas, mainly due to persecution by man. It still occurs in Saudi Arabia, Yemen, Oman and possibly the United Arab Emirates, though the distribution is scattered around the edges

of the Arabian peninsula, with a remnant population thought to exist on the eastern shore of the Dead Sea and in the Negev Desert. Genetic studies have resulted in a proposal that the Arabian leopard should be grouped with seven other subspecies in western Asia as *Panthera pardus saxicolor*, the North Persian leopard. However, area specialists maintain that the Arabian leopard is distinctive, and in the light of new genetic findings its subspecies status has been restored on the basis that populations 'appear to have been isolated for quite a long time, accumulating multiple diagnostic sites that distinguish it from any other subspecies'.

Whatever its classification, it is certain that the Arabian leopard faces a litany of woes, many of which feature on the résumés of other vulnerable cat species: loss of natural prey due to hunting and competition from livestock for grazing; dwindling habitat due to the spread of settlements, tree-cutting and road-building. Add to this the value of the leopard as a hunting trophy or for the price of its skin, as well as the antipathy of man to predators in general, and you have an animal that is trapped, shot and poisoned at every opportunity. Estimates of its surviving population range from around 80 to 250 individuals, with the Yemen home to the bulk of them – though this is probably no more than a good guess. CITES rates the Arabian leopard as Critically Endangered, a status it shares with the Amur and Anatolian subspecies.

The priority for those concerned with the survival of the Arabian leopard is to get base-line information on its distribution and ecology; so far only Oman has a field programme in place using camera traps and satellite telemetry. Photographing the last Arabian leopards has been the ambition of David Willis, a talented Australian artist living in Oman with whom Angie and I became friends during his many visits to the Masai Mara. Like us, David and his family are passionate about wildlife and loved nothing better than to try to catch up with Half-Tail or one of her offspring. David had told me about his quest to photograph the Arabian leopard, a task that made my attempts to record the lives of these secretive creatures in the Mara pale by

Honey with a cub aged three or four months. A hyena killed one of this cub's brothers in a dispute at a kill – the young cheetah did not move away fast enough when challenged.

Lionesses often form a crèche of similar-aged cubs, the most efficient way to raise them.

comparison. His search began in 1991, a year or so after Half-Tail made her first appearance along Fig Tree Ridge and Leopard Gorge. David knew that the Arabian leopard had all but disappeared from the north of Oman, and decided to concentrate his efforts in the high mountain known as Jabal Samhan, one of the most remote areas in the country, where in 1985 four leopards had been trapped to help establish the first captive-breeding centre for Omani mammals. Years later these same animals were used to support a second captive-breeding programme in the Emirate of Sharjah.

On his first week-long safari to Jabal Samhan, David saw ibex, fox and hyrax – his quarry's prey – but no leopard. But he did see signs – scrapes and droppings –

prompting him to return to Jabal Samhan each winter for the next four years. Realizing that photographing a leopard using ordinary techniques was almost impossible, David decided to adopt the methods employed by field biologist Rodney Jackson with snow leopards in the Himalayas. Jackson had finally captured a snow leopard on film using a camera trap activated by a pressure plate. David, ever resourceful and innovative, set about making his own camera trap with solar-powered flash, and installed it on an ibex trail in early 1995. When he retrieved the film three months later he had seven photos of leopards.

David was then joined by biologist Andrew Spalton, who used camera traps and examined leopard scats to try to estimate how many leopards there were, where they moved, what they fed on and if they were breeding successfully. The area they had chosen for their study comprised a system of deep, dry gorges or wadis that twisted and turned through the high mountains, intersected by ancient pathways used since pre-Islamic times by camel caravans that came in search of the much-prized Arabian frankincense – the resin of the *Boswellia sacra* tree. Conditions here are extreme, the land high, hot (in excess of 45°C/113°F in summer) and hyper-arid: by 1995 there had been no rain for six years.

On their second trip together in 1997, Spalton and Willis covered 200km (120 miles) of trails and wadi beds in their search for leopards and suitable sites for camera traps. Occasionally they found scrapes, often containing scats, located under overhangs or at prominent points on trails, left by leopards as a way of marking their home ranges or territories. By analysing hairs in the scats they were able (with help from researchers at the University of Aberdeen) to confirm that the leopards were preying on Nubian ibex, rock hyrax, Arabian gazelle, porcupine and Arabian red-legged partridge. This confirmed the general assumption that

Leopards merge with dappled light so effectively that they can be almost impossible to spot until they move.

leopards prefer to prey on medium-sized ungulates, taking smaller prey to supplement their diet when necessary. Much to their relief, Spalton and Willis found no sign in the scats of camel or goat remains – the domestic stock kept by the local people.

Spalton mounted his camera traps (using infrared beams as a trigger) in old ammunition boxes to prevent loss or damage to his equipment being caused by leopards rubbing their cheeks against the

traps as a form of scent-marking or by striped hyenas chewing the infrared transmitter units. Over the next three years Spalton, often with Willis, hiked into Jabal Samhan every two to three months to service the camera traps. The fact that they rarely got more than one shot per camera per month indicated that leopards were present in low numbers and lived in very large home ranges, so that an individual patrolling its territory passed a given spot only rarely. However, the same

Zawadi on the alert for prey – note the row of five distinct spots below her right eye, making her easy to identify.

his elusive quarry. Not once had he actually seen a leopard.

Buoyed by his success, Spalton got permission to fit global positioning system (GPS) collars, which employ satellites to fix each collared leopard's position. It took seven weeks to capture four leopards (and an Arabian wolf), with a further two leopards caught in early 2002. The smallest, a female, weighed just 17kg (37lb), while the largest was a male of 33 kg (73lb) – nearly double the weight of the female, but still only half that of a full-grown African male. Spalton found that in general the Arabian leopard grows no bigger than 1.3m (4ft 3in) in length from head to tail base, whereas African leopards reach 1.8 m (5ft 10in). The GPS collars weighed 300g (just over 10oz) and were programmed to drop off some months later, allowing location data to be downloaded.

For the moment leopards in the Jabal Samhan Nature Reserve and its southern escarpment seem secure, with a team of rangers patrolling the reserve; conflict with local people is minimal. The hunting and capture of leopards is illegal in Oman, though the collapse of the reintroduced Arabian oryx population in the late 1990s has proved a salutary lesson, which should help to ensure that nothing is taken for granted.

In recent years the main focus of leopard conservation in the Arabian region has been in fostering a captive-breeding programme to act as a safeguard for a viable wild population. But as Andrew Spalton says, 'In Oman, in situ conservation efforts must carry on – for once the leopard has gone from the wild, there will be no return.' By the time the Breeding Centre for Endangered Arabian Wildlife was founded by Sheikh Sultan bin Mohammed al Qassimi, Ruler of Sharjah, in 1996, the population of Arabian leopards had already dipped well below the recommended threshold for a captive-breeding programme to be implemented. After long negotiations seven leopards which had

camera had sometimes taken pictures of both males and females, leading Spalton to deduce that the two sexes occupied overlapping home ranges and avoided one another by using common routes at different times. When Spalton finally removed the traps in November 2000 he had lost cameras to hyenas, rainfall and the effects of monsoon cloud, but had captured more than 200 photographs of been held in captivity in the Yemen for several years were included in the programme, and by the end of 2001 the project totalled 33 leopards (15 males and 18 females), of which half were wild-caught animals to help boost genetic variability. In the Yemen private collectors are willing to pay huge sums of money for a live leopard, and there are a considerable number of such collectors within the Arabian region, raising further anxiety over the wild population, even though such trade is illegal in all the countries concerned.

Once a population drops below a certain level things can become critical, not least because of the effect of inbreeding. One such population, the subspecies *Panthera pardus jarvisi*, was identified in the Judaean Desert and Negev Hills of Israel. In this instance the population had become so unbalanced that there were too many males competing for breeding rights with too few females. Competition among the males was so intense that they continually killed any offspring, and in one instance a male called Hordos killed his mother's two three-month-old cubs. He then mated with his mother and she produced a single male cub which was in turn killed by Hordos' father.

Chui with Light and Dark, providing tourists with the opportunity of a lifetime to watch a mother leopard and her cubs.

In fact both females in this population mated with their own sons, and when one died all the adult males were competing for breeding rights with one female. Between 1984 and 1989, not one cub survived to adulthood, primarily due to the impact of infanticide.

The extreme pressure on this small population was also evident in other ways. An adult female, defeated in a fight with a younger rival, was intimidated into relinquishing most of her territory and moving out with her young son. This older female was seen some time later expelling her nine-month-old daughter from her natal home range. After she became independent the daughter temporarily assumed a substantial part of her mother's range, but was then chased away again by her mother and was never seen in the Judaean Desert again. This highlights the difficulties that small isolated populations face. Denied adequate space and a stable population, the chances of individuals breeding successfully are greatly reduced, leading to an increase in infanticide and inbreeding. Youngsters may be driven away by their mother, long before they are really able to fend for themselves. All these factors combine to produce a precipitous decline in the population.

The Sri Lankan leopard *Panthera pardus kotiya* is another subspecies that has only recently begun to be studied. At the

Zawadi's first litter. Safi (right) is nearing maturity at the time of writing, but her brother was killed by lions when he was six months old.

Zawadi stretching and yawning – typical of a leopard about to become active – at dusk along Leopard Gorge.

beginning of the 20th century the leopard was widespread throughout Sri Lanka (or Ceylon as it then was), and even though the forest cover has since been reduced by more than half, leopards still occur in most of the national parks and in many areas where large tracts of forest and scrub jungle remain. Though no proper census has ever taken place, estimates range from 300–600 leopards, based on prey densities for particular habitats. I first became aware of Sri Lanka's leopard population years ago because the cats were often active during the daytime, making it the perfect area to try to photograph them. As the top predator on the island, leopards do not suffer from competition with tigers, lions or hyenas, and so are free to roam at will, day or night. Though there are scavengers such as sloth bears, mugger crocodiles, wild boars, jackals, mongooses and monitor lizards, these rarely seem to pose a problem, and leopards usually drag kills away from roads and into thick cover, rather than needing to store them in trees. The Sri Lankan leopard is said to be generally larger than other leopards, and to tackle larger prey, perhaps partly due to this lack of

competition from other predators. Its preferred prey is the chital or spotted deer, but it will sometimes tackle almost full-grown buffaloes, as well as small animals such as hares and rats, birds, monitor lizards, pangolins and porcupines.

Studies in Yala National Park suggest that female leopards in Sri Lanka have very small home ranges with considerable overlap, and they are said to be 'more social and tolerant of each other' than leopards observed elsewhere. Smaller home ranges may be related to the plentiful supply of food and the absence of other large predators, allowing the leopards to exist at higher densities. As reported for other leopard populations, males sometimes scavenge from kills made by females, and in one instance a large male fed from a female's kill in her presence and allowed her cub to feed alongside him. Of concern are reports of increasing numbers of leopard skins being seized around Yala and other parts of Sri Lanka, coupled with the demand for leopard bone – a substitute for tiger bone in traditional medicine. Under-funded and under-staffed, the Department of Wildlife struggles to offer adequate protection to the remaining leopards, and poachers rarely receive heavy penalties, often justifying their actions on the grounds that they are protecting their livestock. As everywhere, loss and fragmentation of the leopard's habitat point to an uncertain future, and without detailed scientific research it is impossible to offer proper management.

Angie and I returned to the Mara in early 2003, just before finishing this book. In the intervening months, our friend Paul Goldstein had sent us photographs of two of the leading characters from past series of *Big Cat Diary*. One of them was Amber's daughter Kike, who until now had failed to raise any cubs. Twice she had given birth along the Bila Shaka Lugga, and on both occasions the Marsh Pride had found the den and killed her cubs when they were just

a few weeks old. Kike gave birth for the third time in mid-December 2002, again choosing the Bila Shaka Lugga as a den site. Paul had counted four cubs, and Kike was fortunate in that the Mara had been receiving plenty of rain – not only was the grass long by the time she gave birth, but the soggy conditions prompted the Marsh Pride, who appeared to be prospering, to abandon the heartland of their territory temporarily, following the herds of topis and zebras to the higher ground further east. By the time we saw Kike she had lost one of her cubs, which were now four and a half months old, and had moved with them to an area where we had so often seen her in the past, between Mara Intrepids Camp and Rhino Ridge. Perhaps now that the young cheetahs were old enough to follow their mother they might have a better chance of surviving.

Paul also sent me a photograph of a leopard he had seen close to Leopard Gorge. It was Zawadi's daughter Safi, whom I have yet to see as an adult. As for Zawadi, she was found mating with a shy male at the entrance to Leopard Gorge in late February, and a few days later was spotted around Moses Rock, one of her favourite locations since Half-Tail died and left the area vacant. With a fifth series of *Big Cat Diary* planned for later this year, we are hopeful that by then she will be accompanied by her fifth litter. Zawadi is true to her name, which means gift in Swahili – just as her mother Half-Tail before her had been a gift to everyone who wanted to see wild leopards.

I have often thought about Half-Tail while writing this book, and Angie and I agree that she was a unique character, a wild animal blessed – from our perspective at least – with a temperament that allowed her to accommodate the endless procession of vehicles that searched for her each day in their hope of seeing a leopard. True, everyone wants to see lions and cheetahs too, but finding a leopard adds a different element to a game drive, something

Zawadi with Safi, aged about three months, in early 2000. Leopard cubs start to follow their mother from the age of about eight weeks.

indescribably exciting, the cat of cats. Half-Tail allowed us to indulge that moment of discovery, the knowledge that we were in the presence of a creature whose essence is sublime. Gone were the years of fleeting glimpses of a spotted coat vanishing among cover, the longing to snatch even one good photograph that could be savoured. Here was a leopard who allowed you the chance to absorb her beauty, her secret ways and liquid movements. Half-Tail gave us all of that, and something else besides.

It was one of those mornings when everything just falls into place; an early start full of hope, searching all the familiar places, and then suddenly there she was, right where we hoped she would be, lying

relaxed along a wide branch of one of the giant fig trees that sprout from the cliff face of Fig Tree Ridge. Even with a leopard as obliging as Half-Tail you never took her presence for granted. Having found her, I had to head back to camp, leaving Angie to keep an eye on her in case she moved off to hunt. When I returned a few hours later, she had gone, though Angie was parked in exactly the same spot where I had left her. 'Where's Half-Tail?' I asked. Angie pointed to the side of her car. I backed away until I could just make out Half-Tail wedged in the shade beneath the vehicle, totally trusting.

Vehicles were such a part of Half-Tail's existence that she took them for granted, using them when it suited her as shade or as a blind to hunt from or to scent-mark as

a moveable part of her home range. Angie had never been so close to a wild leopard before and, finding herself alone with no other vehicle to break the spell, she relished the moment, gazing at the sheen of Half-Tail's spotted coat, the brightness of her golden eyes, the length of her long white whiskers. Occasionally Half-Tail looked up, calm and assured, certain, it seemed, that nothing untoward would happen.

As the sun dropped behind a low bank of clouds, she slipped out from beneath the vehicle and stood for a moment, then lowered her forequarters and stretched, a cavernous yawn revealing ivory-coloured teeth. Then she walked away without so much as a backward glance and disappeared from view among the rocks.

Gazetteer of big cat safari destinations

Setting out on a safari to Africa is the high point of many people's lives. For some it will be a journey of just a few weeks; for others it may mean the beginning of a new life, as it was for me when I left London in 1974 and joined a group of other young people travelling overland through Africa.

Most people who come on safari have high expectations, built on visions of wildlife captured in books or on television programmes such as *Big Cat Diary*. But these images can be deceptive, often relying on months or even years of waiting for the right moment, capturing events that happen only rarely. Consequently, when people arrive in the Mara they often expect – rather than hope – to see a leopard lounging in a tree in Leopard Gorge, to experience the thrill of having a cheetah jump on the bonnet of their car, or to watch lions pulling down a buffalo. But there are no guarantees about what you see on safari – just the promise that the experience will change you forever.

The biggest lesson Angie and I learned on our recent safari through southern Africa was to throw away our expectations and enjoy whatever came our way. We had chosen destinations that we hoped would give us the best chance of seeing big cats. Some were famous for leopards or cheetahs, others places where all the big cats were said to be on view. Not all of them lived up to their reputation, not because it was undeserved, but because what we had hoped to see had happened yesterday or last week.

Due to time considerations we visited Namibia, Botswana, Zimbabwe, Zambia and South Africa in one continuous safari in the space of six weeks. The changing seasons can have a huge influence on what you see or don't see, so make sure you are travelling at the right time of the year for each destination when you plan your itinerary. If a place is 'good' for big cats, that implies that there's plenty for them to eat – the antelopes, gazelles, zebras and buffaloes on which they depend. By comparison with these prey species, predators are in the minority, so in looking for them you are guaranteed to find plenty of other animals to feast your eyes on. A safari is so much more than finding big cats. Nevertheless we have chosen places where we have experienced the best big cat watching. Our list is by no means exhaustive. There are many other areas out there waiting to be explored. Though leopards are the focus of this book we have included all three big cats in this review. The Insight guide *African Safari* and the Lonely Planet guides to *Watching Wildlife in East Africa* and *Southern Africa* are a mine of information for safari travellers.

Recommended destinations

Masai Mara National Reserve, Kenya
(1,510 km²/583 sq. miles)

This is one of the best places to see all three big cats, particularly lions. The rainy seasons are mid-October through to December (short rains) and April to June (long rains). The grass is at its longest after the long rains, making it more difficult to find predators, though you are virtually guaranteed to see lions at any time of year. The migration of wildebeest and zebras usually arrives in June or July, with most of the herds returning to the Serengeti by the end of October.

September through to the end of March is our favourite time in the Mara, as the long grass retreats under a wave of animals. The best time to witness the great herds crossing the Mara River is from August to October – so September is a good bet, but no two years are the same. Even when the wildebeest and zebras depart the Mara it is still a beautiful place to visit, and with the grass short (and green during the rains of October–November) it is easier to find predators. The drier the year the better the predator viewing; the grass and bush are eaten back and stripped bare, making it easier to get around and see what is on offer.

The Mara is a birder's paradise, with more than 500 species. For accommodation, try Governor's Camp, Mara Intrepids or Mara River Camp. The Mara Triangle to the west of the river is excellent for cheetahs, though they are found throughout the reserve, and Little Governor's Camp, Olonana and Serena Lodge are among the best places to stay in the Triangle. If you prefer a private tented camp, East African Wildlife Safaris and Abercrombie and Kent are among a number of safari outfitters offering this option in Kenya.

Samburu National Reserve, Kenya
(104 km²/40 sq. miles)

One of the smaller reserves, but what a gem, providing a taste of northern Kenya, with excellent bird life. Any safari to Kenya should include a visit to Samburu. The scenery makes a wonderful contrast to the lush, rolling plains of the Mara, with stark rocky outcrops, dry bush country with towering termite mounds, and the palm-fringed Ewaso Nyiro River. To the south of the river lies Buffalo Springs National Reserve, which is equally good.

The dry seasons are best in Samburu, with plenty of activity around the river and large herds of elephants emerging from the forests to drink and cross. There are Grevy's zebras, gerenuks and reticulated giraffes – dry-country species that you don't find in the Mara.

Samburu and Buffalo Springs are famous for their leopards, and some of the camps and lodges put out bait in the evenings to attract nocturnal visitors. But you are quite likely to see leopards here during the day. There are lions and cheetahs, too, and wild dogs are occasionally seen. Among the best places to stay are Larsens tented camp and Samburu Serena Lodge.

Serengeti National Park, Tanzania
(14,763 km²/5,700 sq. miles)

The Serengeti would be worth a visit even if it didn't have any wildlife. The fact that it does – in the kind of abundance found in few other places – makes this one of our top five wildlife destinations worldwide.

The sheer expanse of the Serengeti plains, particularly in the rainy season when the massed herds of wildebeest and zebras darken the grasslands, is a sight to behold, with lions, hyenas and cheetahs all in attendance. The wildebeest cows give birth to their calves between January and March, so February is a good time to visit. The wildebeest leave the plains and head for the woodlands and water at the beginning of the dry season towards the end of May, streaming in their thousands through the spectacular Moru Kopjes. The more marked the transition between wet and dry seasons, the more dramatic the exodus from the plains. This is when the wildebeest begin their rut, and it is well worth heading for the Seronera area in the centre of the park, which has always been one of Africa's top leopard haunts. They frequently lie up among tall stands of yellow-barked acacia trees along the Seronera Valley or slump contentedly along the broad beam of a sausage tree. Seronera is also a good place to look for lions and cheetahs.

The rugged northern woodlands around Lobo are another good place to visit when the great herds are passing through in the dry season (June–October). Among the best places to stay when the herds are massed on the southern plains are Ndutu Lodge, overlooking Lake Lagarja, and Kusini Camp; with Serengeti Sopa Lodge within easy reach of Moru, Serengeti Serena Lodge a good base in the centre of the park, and Klein's Camp for the Lobo area.

Ngorongoro Crater, Tanzania

(260 km²/100 sq. miles)

The eighth wonder of the world, and certainly worth stopping for two nights, not only for its unique geological features and stunning views, but also as home to some striking black-maned lions. You will be lucky to see cheetahs here, though you might catch sight of a leopard among the forests. The crater is an excellent place to view the endangered black rhino, with the ink-blue backdrop of the crater wall making the perfect scene-setter for wildlife photography. The birdlife is excellent, and the magnificent bull elephants with their long ivory tusks are always a favourite. If you are a keen photographer, or just want to get the best out of your stay, be sure to take a picnic breakfast as well as lunch. The misty morning atmosphere and chances of finding lions on the move make it well worth being out early.

Of the three lodges, Sopa Lodge provides the easiest access to the crater floor, while Ngorongoro Serena Lodge offers 75 rooms, all with crater views. If you just want luxury and fine food, it might almost be worth spending the day in your room, with a view to match, at the Ngorongoro Crater Lodge.

Selous Game Reserve, Tanzania

(43,000 km²/16,600 sq. miles)

Tanzania's southern wilderness is the place to take a walking safari in East Africa. This is 'old' Africa, wild bush country that harbours more than 100,000 buffaloes, nearly 60,000 elephants, the highest density of wild dogs anywhere in Africa and probably the largest single population of lions – with fewer tourists watching them. Even though the lions are not as numerous or as easy to see as in places such as the Mara and Serengeti, a visit to one of the tented camps along the Rufiji River is an ideal starting point for a walking safari. A boat trip along the river to watch giant crocodiles, large pods of hippos and elephants is a must, or you could simply take time out back at camp, to catch up with identifying some of the more than 440 species of birds.

Among the best of the camps are Sand Rivers Selous (particularly for those wanting to walk) and Selous Safari Camp (formerly known as Mbuyuni tented camp). A safari combining a visit to Selous and Ruaha National Park, and either Mahale Mountains or Gombe National Park to see chimpanzees, would be a great adventure away from the hustle and bustle of Tanzania's northern tourist circuit. But if it is easy wildlife watching that you want and your first fix of Africa, then Serengeti, Ngorongoro and Tarangire (1,360km²/525sq. miles), with its magnificent baobabs, large herds of elephants, excellent birdlife and a good chance of seeing lions and leopards, are hard to beat.

South Luangwa National Park, Zambia

(9,050 km²/3,500 sq miles)

Known locally as the Valley, this is where Norman Carr, one of Africa's most experienced safari guides, pioneered walking safaris. The Luangwa River dominates the park, providing a cooling and tranquil element. With the camps and lodges situated along the riverbanks, you can spend hours at a time watching the various animals coming to drink from the veranda of your tent – elephants, buffaloes, pukus, waterbucks, even lions and leopards. The best game-viewing is during winter (May–August) and the dry, hot months from September to November. Game concentrations tend to increase as the dry season progresses, but so too does the temperature. The rains (November–April) are excellent for birding, though most of the lodges and camps close at this time. The density of leopards is exceptional and lions are frequently seen. We visited in September, and during a night game drive – a highlight of any visit to Luangwa – saw one of the leopards that helped to make this area famous. Apart from looking for big cats, we spent many hours photographing elephants drinking and crossing the river, and enjoyed close-up views of the spectacular colonies of carmine bee-eaters that nest in the sandy banks.

There are a number of outfitters offering walking safaris, but Robin Pope Safaris is consistently recommended. The ideal time is probably late June to late September, for a five-day walk with a top guide, staying at mobile tented camps deep in the bush. Robin and Joe Pope also run three of the best permanent camps in the Valley: Nsefu, Tena Tena and Nkwali. A walking safari – even if only for a morning – is a must.

Kafue National Park, Zambia

(22,480 km²/8,680 sq. miles)

The second largest national park in Africa, comprising vast tracts of woodland and savanna bisected by the Kafue River. Surprisingly few people visit Kafue, considering that it is home to large herds of elephants, buffaloes, lions and leopards, and is renowned for its diversity of antelopes, with floodplains brimming with thousands of red lechwes and glimpses of magnificent sables and roans. There are cheetahs and wild dogs here, too, with large prides of lions hunting buffaloes on the Busanga Plain in the north. The animals tend to concentrate around water between July and October, with Busanga best between August and October.

There are only a handful of lodges, adding to the sense of wilderness. Among the best are Ntemwa and Busanga Bush camps, situated in the middle of the plains where lions are often seen; Lufupa Camp is well located for game drives and bush walks, with the chance of seeing leopard on night game drives.

Mana Pools National Park, Zimbabwe

(2,200 km²/850 sq. miles)

It is hard to think of Zimbabwe without planning a visit to the spectacular Victoria Falls and overnighting at the grand Victoria Falls Hotel. This is the place to take a canoe safari down the mighty Zambezi River, which forms the northern boundary of Mana Pools National Park. Hippos, crocodiles, elephants and buffaloes are all easily seen here. Mana is a likely spot to see lions, as is Matusadona National Park, which stretches up from the shores of Lake Kariba, and both offer the chance to walk or canoe, an exciting alternative to being driven around the African bush. John Stevens was one of the pioneers of canoe safaris and is one of Africa's top guides, specializing in walking and canoeing safaris, during which guests stay in mobile tented camps. Musangu and Muchichiri are two pleasant riverside lodges offering permanent accommodation, with Wilderness Safaris' Rukomechi and Chikwenya camps also highly recommended.

If you visit Lake Kariba, then Sanyati Lodge is among the best – you can relax, enjoy the lake and strike out on game drives, walks or fishing trips.

Moremi Game Reserve, Botswana

(3,900 km²/1,505 sq. miles)

The Okavango Delta is a huge oasis, an inland delta of wooded islands and papyrus swamps, whose crystal-clear waters disappear among the Kalahari sands. The delta rivals the Serengeti and Masai Mara as a wildlife spectacle, with excellent lion- and leopard-viewing, and a good chance of seeing cheetahs and wild dogs. The combination of water and wildlife is hard to beat, and the big-game viewing and birding opportunities are virtually limitless. The Moremi Reserve encompasses almost one third of the delta, and includes Chief's Island. The autumn/winter dry season (April–September) is best for wildlife viewing. There is an excellent chance of seeing wild dogs in June and July when they abandon their nomadic wandering for a few months and establish a den. Game-viewing reaches a peak during September and October, when animals congregate around permanent water, though temperatures can be high.

Many lodges close during the rainy season (December–March). There is a huge selection of camps and lodges to choose from, but among the best are Chief's Camp in the Mombo area, and Wilderness Safari's camps, Mombo and Little Mombo.

A visit to the Okavango Delta also offers the possibility of walking safaris, horseback safaris, even elephant-back safaris at Randall Moore's Abu's Camp, and a chance to walk with Doug Groves's elephants at Stanley's Camp. In the north, and bordering Namibia, Chobe National Park (11,700 km²/4,520 sq. miles) is home to large prides of lions and huge herds of buffaloes, and offers river trips to watch elephants crossing the Chobe River. In the west of the park, the Linyanti Marsh and Savuti areas are famous for their lion-viewing, though it can be very seasonal. Chobe is a good place to visit en route to Victoria Falls, stopping over at Chobe Chilwero Lodge.

Okonjima and the Africat Foundation, Namibia

(135 km²/52 sq. miles)

Namibia is home to more cheetahs than any other African country, with perhaps 3,000 of these elegant cats. But 90 per cent are found on private ranchland, where they often run into conflict with ranchers. Lise Hanssen and her team at the Africat Foundation have dedicated themselves to working with ranchers to lessen conflict with predators, removing animals that are trapped and might otherwise be shot or poisoned. They work mainly with cheetahs and leopards, but also with servals, caracals and the occasional lion, supporting a number of research and education projects.

The Hanssens have turned the family home at Okonjima ranch into comfortable guest accommodation, providing visitors with the chance to visit the Africat Foundation and meet some of the cheetahs. Photographers will find plenty of interest here, and a visit to the leopard blind in the evening is an experience not to be missed.

The Cheetah Conservation Fund (CCF), Otjiwarongo, Namibia

CCF was the brainchild of Laurie Marker and Daniel Kraus, and is dedicated to the long-term survival of the cheetah through research and education. Laurie and her team are at the hub of cheetah conservation and, like the Africat Foundation, work closely with ranchers, providing a home for orphaned cheetahs trapped on ranchland. CCF has pioneered the use of guard dogs to help farmers reduce stock losses to predators, and has placed well over 120 Anatolian Shepherd dogs with farmers. Where possible wild-caught adult cheetahs are relocated. The excellent Visitor Education Centre at CCF is open to the public.

To see wild cheetahs in Namibia, the best option is to visit Etosha National Park (22,270 km²/8,600 sq. miles). Natural springs and artificial waterholes (such as the Okaukuejo waterhole) dotted along the southern edge of the stark Etosha Pan at the heart of the park provide the focal point for game-viewing, attracting large numbers of animals, such as wildebeest, zebras, springboks, gemsboks and elands. Though all three big cats are found here, there is no guarantee that you will see them. If big cats are the priority and time is short then perhaps this is not the place for you; otherwise it is memorable.

Namib-Naukluft Park, Namibia

(49,754 km²/19,210 sq. miles)

This enormous wilderness stretches from Luderitz in the south to Swakopmund in the north. Not the place to see big cats, but as a safari destination it is a world apart, a vast moonscape with towering dunes, which are transformed when the summer rains come – if they come – in December to February. The extraordinary creeping welwitschia plants are endemic to the Namib and can live for more than 2,000 years. Sossusvlei Mountain Lodge in the adjoining Namib Rand Nature Reserve, and Wilderness Sossusvlei Camp are among the best, offering a variety of activities including day trips to the towering dunes of Sossusvlei. There is even a star-gazing safari with the help of a giant telescope at Mountain Lodge – not to be missed.

Kruger National Park, South Africa

(19,480 km²/7,520 sq. miles)

This is South Africa's premier national park, with more mammal and bird species than any other park in the country. All of the 'big five' can be found here – lions, leopards, buffaloes, rhinos and elephants – as well as cheetahs and wild dogs, with the southern area of the park offering the greatest variety of landscape and the best game-viewing. The one big limitation has always been that you are confined to tarmac roads. However, the parks authorities have recently put out to tender a number of private concessions, where off-road driving and walking safaris from small camps and lodges will add a whole new dimension to a safari in Kruger. Game-viewing is best during winter (May–October), when animals concentrate at water sources. The rainy season is from October to March.

Sabi Sands Game Reserve, South Africa (including Londolozi and Mala Mala)

(650 km²/250 sq. miles)

There are a number of private game reserves clustered along the western boundary of the Kruger that are no longer separated from it by fencing. These offer excellent opportunities for big cat enthusiasts, and are particularly worth a visit if your passion is leopards. The most famous is Londolozi (130km²/50sq. miles), which has been transformed by John and Dave Varty since they took over the lodge in the early 1970s and restored the area to its former glory. Also well worth a visit is Mala Mala – both of these virtually guarantee leopard sightings. When we visited Londolozi we saw three different leopards on five separate occasions, as well as three magnificent male lions and plenty of cubs, white rhinos, elephants and two glorious kudu bulls.

Night game drives are a feature at all the lodges, and a good way to see leopards, though the rangers work hard to track them down during daytime as well, with off-the-road driving the norm. Cheetahs and wild dogs are not uncommonly seen. Ngala, Sabi Sabi, Singita and Idube lodges are all recommended.

Phinda Resource Reserve, South Africa

(180 km²/70 sq. miles)

Lions and cheetahs have been introduced to this private game reserve, and it is certainly a good place to photograph them – particularly cheetahs, which are almost guaranteed. But getting a clear view of them usually depends on being able to drive off-road, and this is restricted after annual burning, so be sure to check first. All the 'big five' are here, and leopards are quite often seen. Winter (May–October) is the dry season and the best time for clear sightings. Accommodation is in four luxury lodges. Phinda offers a number of extensions. You can opt to walk in search of black rhino in the adjacent Mkuzi Game Reserve, dive on the east coast coral reefs or fly over Greater St Lucia Wetland Park.

Further Information:

Websites

African National Parks
HYPERLINK
http://www.newafrica.com/nationalparks/
Africat (Lise Hanssen's project)
HYPERLINK http://www.africat.org/
Cheetah Conservation Fund
(Laurie Marker's project)
HYPERLINK http://www.cheetah.org
Big Cats Online
dialspace.dial.pipex.com/agarman/bco/ver4.htm
Big Cat Research
www.bigcats.com/
IUCN Cat Specialist Group
lynx.uio.no/catfolk
The Lion Research Centre (lions of the Serengeti
and Ngorongoro Crater)
HYPERLINK http://www.lionresearch.org
Friends of Conservation
(conservation body involved in the Mara)
HYPERLINK http://www.foc-uk.com

Tour Operators

Abercrombie and Kent
(East and southern Africa)
HYPERLINK http://www.abercrombiekent.co.uk
Afro Ventures (East and southern Africa)
HYPERLINK http://www.afroventures.com
Conservation Corporation Africa
(East and southern Africa)
HYPERLINK http://www.ccafrica.com
East African Wildlife Safaris (Kenya)
HYPERLINK mailto:eaws@kenyaweb.com
Gibb's Farm Safaris (Tanzania)
HYPERLINK mailto:ndutugibbs@nabari.co.tz
John Stevens Safaris
(Zimbabwe canoe/walking safaris)
HYPERLINK mailto:bushlife@hare.iafrica.com
Okavango Tours and Safaris
(Botswana)
HYPERLINK http://www.okavango.com
Richard Bonham Safaris
(Tanzania – Selous specialist)
HYPERLINK
mailto:Bonham.Luke@swiftkenya.com
Robin Pope Safaris
(Zambia – Luangwa Valley specialist)
HYPERLINK mailto:popesaf@zamnet.zm
Wilderness Safaris
(southern Africa specialists)
HYPERLINK mailto:outposts@usa.net
Governor's Camp
(Kenya/Masai Mara tented camps)
HYPERLINK mailto:info@governorscamp.com
Worldwide Journeys and Expeditions
(African safari specialists)
www.worldwidejourneys.co.uk

Bibliography

It would have been impossible to write this book without leaning heavily on the work of other authors. We're particularly grateful to Luke Hunter, who was incredibly generous with his time, providing us with invaluable information on Africa's big cats, as well as many contacts among predator researchers working in southern Africa. Here in Nairobi, Judith Rudnai kindly shared her excellent library of books and articles with us. Thanks are also due to Gus Mills at Kruger Park in South Africa for his fund of knowledge on Africa's large predators and providing copies of scientific articles; Lise Hanssen of the Africat Foundation (thank you, Lise, for sending copies of Flip Stander's excellent leopard papers) and the Hanssen family at Okonjima in Namibia, who were helpful and welcoming. So too were Laurie Marker and everyone at the Cheetah Conservation Fund. Our Nairobi neighbours, Esmund Bradley-Martin and his wife Chryssee, were a mine of information on matters relating to wildlife conservation, and generously allowed us access to back issues of *Cat News*, the newsletter of the Species Survival Commission (IUCN), which I would recommend highly to anyone with a passion for the world's wild cats.

Ted Bailey's book *The African Leopard* is essential reading for leopard enthusiasts, and the accounts of leopard behaviour written by Lex Hess (formerly a ranger at Londolozi), and filmmakers Dale Hancock and Kim Wolhuter at Mala Mala provided us with many insights. We are only too well aware of the dangers of interpreting the work of others, particularly when trying to present information gleaned from scientific papers in a 'popular' way. Accordingly, while we are indebted to the following authors, they remain blameless for any inaccuracies in our text, and we apologize for the inevitable simplifications in interpreting their work.

Adamson, J. *Born Free: the full story*, Pan Books: London 2000
Ames, E. A *Glimpse of Eden*, Collins: London 1968
Bailey, T.N. *The African Leopard: ecology and behavior of a solitary felid*, Columbia University Press: New York 1993
Bertram, B.C.R. *Pride of Lions*, J.M.Dent: London 1978
————— *Lions*, Colin Baxter Photography: Grantown-on-Spey 1998
Bothma, J du P. and Walker, C. *Larger Carnivores of the African Savannas*, J. L. van Schaik Publishers: Pretoria 1999
Estes, R.D. T*he Behavior Guide to African Mammals: including hoofed mammals, carnivores, primates*, University of California Press: Oxford, England 1991
Grzimek, B., & Grzimek, M. *Serengeti Shall Not Die*, Hamish Hamilton: London 1960
Hall-Martin, A, & Bosman, P. *Cats of Africa*, Swan Hill Press, an imprint of Airlife Publishing: Shrewsbury 1997
Hancock, D. *A Time with Leopards*, Black Eagle Publishing: Cape Town 2000
Hess, L. *The Leopards of Londolozi*, Struik, Winchester, an imprint of Struik Publishers (Pty) Ltd: Cape Town 1991
Hunter, L.T.B. 'The Quintessential Cat.' *Africa: environment and wildlife*. Vol. 7 (2): 32-41 1999
————— 'Fighting tooth and claw: the future of Africa's magnificent cats.' *Africa Geographic*. Vol. 9 (5): 46-56 2001
Jackman, B.J. 'Cat-watching, Africa: lions, leopards and cheetahs: where to see them', *BBC Wildlife*, Vol.19, No.2 2001
Jackman, B.J., & Scott, J.P. *The Marsh Lions*, Elm Tree Books: London 1982
—————*The Big Cat Diary*, BBC Books: London 1996
Jackson, P. (ed) *Cat News*, the newsletter of the Species Survival Commission (IUCN) No.36 Spring 2002 and No.37 Autumn 2002
Jordan, W. *Leopard*, Hodder Wayland, an imprint of Hodders Children's Books 2001
Kingdon, J. *East African Mammals: an atlas of evolution in Africa*, Vol.3, part A (Carnivores), Academic Press: London 1977
Kumara, J. 'Island Leopard (Sri Lanka)', *BBC Wildlife*, Dec 2001
Macdonald, D. *The Velvet Claw: a natural history of the carnivores*, BBC Books: London 1992
Mellon, J. *African Hunter*, Cassell: London 1975
Mills, G., & Harvey, M. *African Predators*, Struik Publishers: South Africa 2001
Moss, C. *Portraits in the Wild: animal behaviour in East Africa*, Elm Tree Books: London 1989
Myers, N. 1973. 'The spotted cats and the fur trade' in R. L. Eaton, ed., *The World's Cats. Vol. 1, Ecology and Conservation*, pp. 276–326. Winston, OR: World Wildlife Safari
—————1976. 'The leopard *Panthera pardus* in Africa'. IUCN monogr. no. 5
Neff, N.A. *The Big Cats: the paintings of Guy Coheleach*, Harry N. Abrams: New York 1982
Nowell, K., & Jackson, P. *Wild Cats: status survey and conservation action plan*, IUCN/SSC Cat Specialist Group, IUCN: Gland, Switzerland.
Pocock, R. I. 'The Leopards of Africa'. *Proc. Zool. Soc.* London, 543 1932
Schaller, G.B. *The Serengeti Lion: a study of predator-prey relations*, University of Chicago Press: Chicago 1972
—————*Serengeti: a kingdom of predators*, Collins: London 1973

Scott, J.P. *The Leopard's Tale*, Elm Tree Books: London 1985

————*The Great Migration*, Elm Tree Books: London 1988

————*Painted Wolves: wild dogs of the Serengeti–Mara*, Hamish Hamilton: London 1991

————*Kingdom of Lions*, Kyle Cathie: London 1992

————*Dawn to Dusk: a safari through Africa's wild places*, BBC Books: in association with Kyle Cathie: London 1996

————*Jonathan Scott's Safari Guide to East African Animals (revised and updated by Angela Scott)*, Kensta: Nairobi 1997

————*Jonathan Scott's Safari Guide to East African Birds (revised and updated by Angela Scott)*, Kensta: Nairobi 1997

Scott, J. P., & Scott, A. 'Death on the rocks (infanticide in leopards)', *BBC Wildlife*, Vol.16 No.4 April 1998

————*Mara–Serengeti: a photographer's paradise*, Fountain Press: London 2000

————*Big Cat Diary: Lion*, HarperCollins: London 2002

Seidensticker, J., & Lumpkin, S. (eds) *Great Cats: majestic creatures of the wild*, Merehurst, by arrangement with Weldon Owen

Shales, M. *African Safari*, Discovery Communications: 2000

Spalton, A. 'Chasing the leopard's tale (Arabian leopards)', *BBC Wildlife*, August 2002

Stander, P. E. 'The ecology of asociality in Namibian leopards'. *J. Zool.*, London, 242, 343-364 1997

Stander, P. E. 'Field age determination of leopards by tooth wear'. *Afr. J. Ecol.* Vol 35 May 1997

Sunquist, M, and Sunquist, F. *Wild Cats of the World*, University of Chicago Press: Chicago and London 2002

Turnbull-Kemp, P. *The Leopard*, Howard Timmins: Cape Town 1967

Turner, A., & Anton, M. *The Big Cats and their Fossil Relatives: an illustrated guide to their evolution and natural history*, Columbia University Press: New York 1997

Uphyrkina, O et al. 'Phylogenetics, genome diversity and origin of modern leopards'. *Molecular Ecology* 10: 2617-2633. 2001

Acknowledgements

We have received such generous support from so many individuals and companies that it is possible to mention only a few of them here.

We would like to thank the governments of Kenya and Tanzania for allowing us to live and work in the Serengeti–Mara, and to acknowledge the assistance of Tanzania National Parks, and both the Narok and Trans Mara County Councils, who administer the Masai Mara National Game Reserve. Over the years Senior Wardens John Naiguran, Simon Makallah, Michael Koikai, Stephen Minis and James Sindiyo in the Mara, and David Babu and Bernard Maregesi in the Serengeti have all been helpful and supportive of our projects, as have Brian Heath and Jonny Baxendale of the Mara Conservancy (Mara Triangle).

Thanks to everyone involved in *Big Cat Diary* (BCD), both here in Kenya and at the Natural History Unit (NHU) in Bristol. To 'field commander' Keith Scholey and series producer Fiona Pitcher, for supporting the idea of this series of books, and to Keith and his wife Liz, and Robin and Elin Hellier, for welcoming us into their homes whenever we visit the NHU. The success of BCD relies on people working together, and as much as anyone Mandy Knight, production manager of series 1 to 4, epitomizes the combination of professionalism and big-heartedness which makes working on BCD such a privilege and pleasure.

Rosamund Kidmund-Cox, editor of *BBC Wildlife* magazine, has been a good friend and great supporter of our work over the years, and helped us believe that there was room for yet more books on Africa's big cats.

Myles Archibald at HarperCollins commissioned this series of three titles featuring Africa's big cats, beginning with *Lion* (we are now hard at work on the final book *Cheetah*). Myles' enthusiasm for the project helped to spur us on. Helen Brocklehurst, our editor at HarperCollins, has been a pleasure to work with, full of optimism and new ideas, and Liz Brown, our designer, managed to add her own brand of creative flare in record time.

Caroline Taggart has edited all but one of our books, but even someone as unflappable as Caroline realized that once again she was going to have to call on all her considerable editing skills – and an uncanny ability to make her authors feel that anything is possible – if we were to complete *Leopard* on time. Thank you again.

Mike Shaw, who was for many years our literary agent at Curtis Brown, always provided a safe pair of hands and we wish him a long and happy retirement. His former assistant Jonathan Pegg has agreed to take on the role of our agent and has been wonderfully supportive, managing our affairs with great charm and professionalism.

Our wildlife photographs are held by three picture libraries: NHPA, ImageState and Getty Images. Tim Harris and his team at NHPA generously allowed us to rifle the leopard files at short notice for this book, as did Diana Leppard at ImageState and Helen Gilks at the Nature Picture Library who hold some of Angie's pictures.

Both Angie and I have family living overseas who have been an unfailing source of help and encouragement. Now that my sister Caroline has moved from England to sunny Portugal, my brother Clive and his wife Judith have kindly inherited the boxes of books and slides that used to live at Caroline's house in Inkpen. Angie's mother Joy still lives in England but sadly hasn't enjoyed the best of health recently, and her brother David and wife Mishi now live in France. Her cousin Richard Thornton, his wife Gay and their daughter Bridget and husband Bill kindly found space for more of our possessions at short notice. We miss them all.

Pam Savage and Michael Skinner have taken us under their wing these past few years, offering advice and reassurance when needed, and allowing us the freedom of their home in London. It is difficult to know how to thank friends like that adequately, though dedicating this book to Pam will perhaps go some small way towards recording our gratitude to her for many kindnesses over the years. Cissy and David Walker have been equally forthcoming with their generosity and good fellowship.

Frank and Dolcie Howitt continue to be the best of neighbours to us here in Nairobi, and are very dear friends.

Many other people have provided us with a second home during our visits to England over the years, particularly Pippa and Ian Stewart-Hunter in London, Brian and Annabelle Jackman in Dorset, Dr Michael and Sue Budden in Buckinghamshire, Ken and Lois Kuhle and Martin and Avril Freeth in London, and Charles and Lindsay Dewhurst in West Sussex, who have been such caring and generous guardians to our son David during his schooldays in England. They are all wonderful hosts and friends who put up with our comings and goings with admirable tolerance.

We have shared some remarkable times with our good friends Neil and Joyce Silverman in Africa, Antarctica and their beautiful home in Florida. They have helped us in many ways over the years, and are always there when we need them.

Carole Wyman has been a loyal and generous friend to Angie since they met in Kenya many years ago, and is godmother to our son David. Carol is an individual of rare qualities, and our only regret is that we see so little of her and her husband Karma.

Jock Anderson of East African Wildlife Safaris continues to be a great friend to our family. He gave me the chance to live at Mara River Camp 27 years ago, a gift of such magnitude that I shall never forget his role in making it possible. Stephen Masika, Jock's office messenger, still keeps track of correspondence and renews licences for us with unfailing efficiency.

Aris, Justin and Dominic Grammaticus have been generous in allowing us to base ourselves at Governor's Camp, and Pat and Patrick Beresford and their staff at Governor's Workshop somehow manage to keep us on the road, regardless of the damage we inflict on our Toyota Landcruiser.

Finally, we would like to acknowledge the invaluable help of Shigeru Ito of Toyota East Africa, Allan Walmsley, formerly of Lonrho Motors East Africa, Canon Camera Division (UK), John Buckley and Anna Nzomo at Air Kenya, Mehmood and Shaun Quraishy at Spectrum Colour Lab (Nairobi), Pankaj Patel of Fuji Kenya, Jan Mohamed of Serena Hotels and David Leung, the Canon Camera specialist at Goodmayes Road, Ilford (UK), all of whom make life in the bush tenable through their ongoing support.

We are truly fortunate in being able to follow our passion as a career. But the joy that this brings pales alongside the inspiration and love we derive from our children Alia and David. May their lives be equally blessed.

Index

Page numbers in *italic* refer to illustrations